ESSAYS FOR SENIOR CLASSES

Published by
Lotus Press Publishers & Distributors

ESSAYS FOR SENIOR CLASSES

A.K. Pillai

4735/22, Prakash Deep Building,
Ansari Road, Daryaganj,
New Delhi - 110002

Lotus Press : Publishers & Distributors
Unit No. 220, 2nd Floor, 4735/22, Prakash Deep Building,
Ansari Road, Darya Ganj, New Delhi- 110002
Ph.: 23280047, 98118-38000
• E-mail : lotuspress1984@gmail.com
www.lotuspress.co.in

Essays for Senior Classes

ISBN: 978-81-8382-249-7

Printed & Published by : **Lotus Press Publisher & Distributors,** New Delhi-02

PREFACE

Senior Essays is a collection of higher level of consciousness essays which provides knowledge at higher level and wider scale. The major goal of various essays in this book is to serve as preliminary explorations an senior thesis topics.

This book consists of enormous valued essays on several topics like qualities of a citizen, the golden age of youth, the work of a newspaper reporter and many more. Though, we have tried hard to explore the advantages and disadvantages that occur due to our day-to-day activities and to make children aware of their beneficial and harmful impacts. The basic aim of the book is to make children learn about, and essay writing, consisting of a quality write up and to enlarge their knowledge about the world around to make them learn how to move a step forward from a junior to a senior level.

–Author

CONTENTS

1. QUALITIES OF A GOOD CITIZEN

A good citizen is one who is a good person. There seems to be no scope for differentiating between the two – a weak or bad person cannot be a good citizen and it holds the truth other way round also. It is man's day-to-day behaviour and his day-to-day virtues which count and contribute to his character. A good citizen is one whose behaviour is consistent with the canons of self-respect and social justice and should be reliable both on peace and war.

The first and foremost quality asked of good citizen is patriotism. He should have genuine love for his country and a sense of involvement in his day-to-day affairs, economic policies and international relationships. All this cannot be achieved overnight: it is the product of good training, good heritage and various other factors that contribute towards patriotic feelings.

The first among these is the right kind of upbringing. If a child hears only stories of betrayal and pays attention towards discussion on various methods of making easy money, he is unlikely to imbibe any good qualities. The hand that rocks the cradle shapes the world. Honesty, integrity and self-respect are the qualities that can only be nurtured at home. These form the foundation of good citizenship.

The home and the family are miniature groups. If a person gets his values and priorities honestly while living in these, he will prove to be a good citizen. A good citizen must put the interest of his country before his own personal interest and should not enter into any contract or design which may prove harmful for the interest of his country and must do his share of work and responsibilities.

These are the qualities which add up to strength and character. A good citizen puts his country before self interest. There are many jobs which if correctly performed add to the national progress. Industries, when expanded properly, become a part of national wealth. They provide opportunities for employment and development. A farmer, a teacher, a soldier, every individual is important in his own role. He who loves his country puts his heart in his job and does it to the best of his ability. A good citizen must stay away from anti-social activities like smuggling and corruption.

The passive virtue of being anti-social is not only important but also the positive quality of asserting oneself; being fearless enough to point out and face anti-social elements is valuable. It is not enough to slink out of their way and say that we are not concerned. Courage is not only physical but also moral; one does not require it only when faced by an enemy or in a moment of crisis but in day-to-day decisions and activities. Courage is intimately connected with self-respect. A man who is servile and can stoop down to any level will not be brave and honest. A man who has a great deal of self-respect will be courageous in the face of odds.

2. THE GOLDEN AGE OF YOUTH

I am certainly not experiencing "golden" days in my life as a youth. Furthermore, many of my friends' complaints seem to attest that their experiences of youth roughly match up with mine, that is, life as a youth is tough!

Firstly, being young automatically means that I have limited knowledge and no job skills, which means that no one will employ me for any worthwhile job. This means, clearly and simply, "No Independent Income". Now, it is undeniable that without money, you become severely limited in your options. You cannot buy anything, nor go anywhere or do anything. Obviously, this is a problem for me.

Unable to function without cash, I have to rely on my parents for financial help. Unable to buy a car, I have to rely on them for transport facility. Unable to buy a house, I have to rely on them for accommodation. This means, theoretically, that my parents are my Supreme Commanders. When they tell me to jump, I have to do as they say. In such a situation, I am deprived of the vital human rights.

Secondly, as long as you are not too old or too ill to walk, people will always be measuring you by your achievements. This is especially true for people in their youth. Parents, teachers, society and the government love to gauge us scholastically, physically, socially, morally and in whatever means they can think of. Thus, school examinations become so important that many of us will study hours on end to perform well in them.

Actually, the pressure on us to perform well at all times is great. The pressure from our family gets stronger as we grow older. Since we started schooling, our parents have been comparing our test results with those of the children of their friends, who happen to be equally goal-orientated parents. In fact, since we were born, our parents have been comparing the ages at which we first started talking, walking, our kiddy IQ test results and such other traps for vainglory. If I were a piece of chicken, I'd consider myself "Kentucky Fried", not because I was "spicy" or "original" but because I have been chopped into pieces, tenderised, pressure-cooked and well-fried.

Then, there is the question of romance. Practically speaking, youth is the worst time to get romantically attached, because, as was earlier explained, we lack the time and money to maintain a special boy-girl relationship.

Yet, during our youth, we are at our peak; physically, in looks we are the most attractive. Furthermore, our hormones are swinging about wildly as we mature sexually. Unfortunately, this causes us to be more prone of getting involved into romantic relationships, which leads to heartache and cause us to perform badly in our examinations. I think that the government should have chosen a better time to set all the major examinations than at this time–don't you think so?

So, youth is a traumatic time. It is definitely not "golden". In my opinion, the idea of "The Golden Age of Youth" must have been an illusion dreamt up by fools. Perhaps we should call it the "Iron Pyrite (Fool's Gold) Age of Youth".

3. IMPORTANCE OF VOCATIONAL GUIDANCE

The present for us is one of special significance and an era of changes. New patterns emerge and new ideals are proposed. The era of independence and the attendant changes have radically altered the context in which the school pursues its major aims. Change which symbolises progress demands an urgent reorientation of the attitudes of the students towards jobs. In the process of mopping up the cobwebs of prejudice against blue-collar jobs and dissemination of occupational information, the school has to pay an important role.

In past, in the whole complex and complicated field of education there was no aspect neglected than vocational guidance? Thanks to the dynamism and foresight of the education authorities, the student has ample opportunities to gain sufficient occupational information to equip him to choose a job that is consistent with his aptitude and general ability. The student who leaves school without having a vague idea of job that he would take up is apt to fall into a taste of Flux and there is the danger that he may choose the wrong job and so despair. Today, the school-leaver would have at least a vague idea of the job that he intends taking up.

Each year, there are large numbers of school-leavers. It is important, therefore, that young citizens should be guided to the right career when they leave school. A youth who plunges blindly into a job for which he is not suited, has no interest, can very aptly be likened to a round peg in a square hole. No country can afford to have such a state of affairs. It is, thus, of paramount importance that every individual is properly guided in choicing a career so that he can contribute his maximum to the society.

About two-third of a man's life is spent in work even in these days of automation. And, the choice of career is certainly a delicate issue for him. Making the wrong choice can land him in a world of endless frustration! Very often, the first job that a school-leaver gets is the one he has to stay at throughout his working career. So, unless he is content with and suited to the job he has, he will never be happy. Vocational guidance is thus important as its fundamental aim is to help the individual in choosing a suitable career according to his aptitudes, interests and training.

The industries are confronted with the problem of shortage of skilled workers. This shortage of trained man-power to meet our industrialisation programme is a reflection of the inadequacies and shortcomings of a past education which was ill-equipped to prepare young school-leavers with the necessary knowledge and skills for employment in industries. This problem, however, is further aggravated by certain values developed from the colonial era when many were groomed for clerical positions and white-collar jobs. The traditional prejudice against blue-collar jobs is still firmly entrenched. The reluctance to prepare for blue-collar jobs means an inadequate number of skilled workers and technicians. Such ingrained negative attitudes towards manual jobs indeed necessitate vocational guidance in schools.

4. THE IMPORTANCE OF UNIVERSITY EDUCATION FOR WOMEN

University education as compared to the general education in the secondary school stands as a class apart. Whereas the aim of the secondary school education is to give general knowledge to all and the university education helps specialisation in various faculties. Besides this, of course, there is the life which is lived by the alumni which goes to improve the character and outlook of the student-life. It was the tradition of great universities like Oxford, Cambridge and Harvard that their dons received not only a degree but also a hallmark of quality.

Till recently university education was the preserve of menfolk and to see women in the university was strange. But now the universities have opened their doors for women students. There is no department of study where women do not compete with men. Even the faculties like engineering and law which were entirely men's preserve, have yielded to women. Women have understood the need for higher education and there has been an awakening among them.

It will be worthwhile to study the importance of university education for women. There are many influences working in favour of women seeking higher education. First and foremost is political awakening. In all countries women have been enfranchised and are entering politics in large numbers. Many women have worked and are working as ministers today. So politics gave incentive and impetus for women seeking higher education. Politics helped them, in fact, to shake off the feminine reserved nature and they came out of the cloistered life.

Further, old customs and traditions that kept women bound to their kitchen and the thought that sewing and stitching were their occupations, were broken. Mingling with young men in the colleges was no more hindrance or an anathema in women seeking higher education. Women have now begun to seek career and marriage is no more considered as be-all and end-all of their lives. To be successful in a career higher education was naturally sought after. Further, the value of higher education for women began to get recognition, though slowly.

University education for women has its own values that renders them as useful citizens, helpful wives, mothers and very often useful neighbours and sometimes good social workers. Since women are equal to men according to any modern constitution, they form the major bulk of the electorate.

Children are the ones that gain really, because an educated mother looks after the education of her children. Yet there is another value which is derived from their university education apart from entering a career in times of need, such as the desertion of the husband, when the woman can stand on her own feet and look after her children.

But wisdom calls for a different type of curriculum for women. The education which women get at the university should be complementary to what menfolk get there, rather than being a rival to them. So far, this aspect has not been fully appreciated, though it is so apparent.

5. THE WORK OF A NEWSPAPER REPORTER

Newspapers are the windows of the world that give citizens an idea of what has happened and what is happening around. The success of a newspaper depends on how swift and reliable the news it gives to the public. There are times when details of news are anxiously awaited and this is where newspapers must help, and if this is done ably then that paper is popular. There are many great newspapers in the world like the *Times of London, New York Times, Manchester Guardian, Le Monde, Times of India,* the *Hindu* and so on. These papers depend on the reporters and their representatives for the news.

A reporter may be permanent or special. Big papers have their permanent representatives in important cities. A reporter must be well-qualified and proficient in the language he uses and must have a university degree, especially in literature and humanities, though there are reporters who are proficient in sciences. He must have an eye for news and report it in an attractive way. He must have taste for many kinds of arts that help to give a critical view. He must be an outgoing sociable man. A reporter should have thorough knowledge of current history, and something about the personalities on the scene. He should also have a flair for language.

A reporter should be able to cover the day-to-day incidents quickly. The reports must be genuine and reliable; otherwise, very soon the paper will lose its name. He must be capable of meeting important persons and if needed, to interview them. He must be capable of getting local news so that the public will be aware of local happenings. Reports on the general election or budget session of the Parliament may be important. A reporter may be able to give an inkling as to why certain things are happening the way they do or are likely to take place. Sometimes it may be investigative reporting. This is very important because it helps to alert people and to warn those who are the wrongdoers. In fact, a good reporter may help to sway the public opinion.

A reporter should also be a good photographer in order to grasp the best of a person or an incident. A quick correct flash of an important event will be valued very much.

A reporter has to travel. He must have an idea of what different people do and live in different countries without affecting the philosophy and stand taken by his paper. His reporting must be unbiased.

A reporter is responsible for the paper he represents. The paper's name and fame depends on the news. The reporter must be aware of his responsibilities.

6. DEVALUATION OF CURRENCY

Currency is the easiest form to settle bargains in trade and commerce, whether it be in a simple, elementary level between a seller and buyer, or in a complicated level between one country and another. Each country has her own currency and it is valued in terms of an international currency such as the pound sterling or American dollar. This linking is purely a matter of convention and convenience and this helps in carrying on international trade directly with Great Britain or the U.S.A. or indirectly with other countries through them. The importance arises in settling payments for exports and imports and for services.

The financing authority of a country can change the value of their currency in relation to other currencies according to the strength or weakness of her balance of payment. This is a kind of jugglery and requires a lot of tact and prudence. About two decades ago, the American dollar was worth about $ 3 in Singapore, which meant that a dollar worth of goods was equivalent to three Singapore dollars worth of goods.

Why did they do it? Though it is quite complicated, it can be explained this way. Suppose there are more foreign goods going in, then in terms of the US dollars the things will become costly and so it will discourage people from going in for foreign services. That would mean that the internal economy could be geared to better production. If it is luxury goods people getting from other countries, then the increase in cost will discourage them from going in for the foreign products like the motor car, etc. The internal prices will go high but production will rise. While this may discourage internal consumption, a foreigner may find it cheaper to buy in his currency; thus the effect of devaluation may be to boost up exports and, in fact, the monopoly items may have a facelift and this will encourage an expansion of export trade, and so there will be new markets established. The foreign investor will find it advantageous to invest in the devaluing country. His investment will get an artificial boost. Thus devaluation would encourage the flow of foreign money into the devaluing country. In terms of foreign currency taking the money out would not be advantageous. That money would, perforce, be ploughed back into the country's economy.

Indirectly it means that the people would have to work hard. Foreign goods may become dearer. It would mean incentive for more production. But devaluation is to be handled very carefully, otherwise, it would wreck the economy of the country, shake the confidence of the foreign investor and also the prestige of the country concerned.

7. UNEMPLOYMENT

India as a nation is faced with the massive problem of unemployment. Unemployment can be defined as a state of worklessness for a man fit and willing to work. It is a condition of involuntary and not voluntary idleness.

The problem of unemployment has become colossal. Various problems have caused this problem. There are individual factors like age, vocational unfitness and physical disabilities which restrict the people. External factors include technological and economic factors. There is enormous increase in the population. Every year India adds to her population afresh. More than this, every year about 5 million people become eligible for securing jobs. The business field is subject to ups and downs of the trade cycle and globalization. Economic depression or sick industries are often closed down, compelling their employees to become unemployed. Technological advancement contributes to economic development. But unplanned and uncontrolled growth of technology is causing havoc on job opportunities. The computerisation and automation has led to technological unemployment. Strikes and lockouts have become an inseparable aspect of the industrial world today. Due to these, industries often face economic losses and production comes down. Since workers do not get any salary or wages during the strike period, they suffer from economic hardships. They become permanently or temporarily unemployed. Today, young people are not ready to take jobs which are considered to be socially degrading. Our educational system has its own irreparable defects and contribution to unemployment is an open truth. Our education does not prepare the minds of the young generation to become self-employed, on the contrary, it makes them dependent on government vacancies which are hard to come.

Our State right from the beginning of Five Year Plans has introduced several employment-generating schemes and programmes over the years, but in the absence of proper implementation and monitoring have failed to achieve the required targets. Recently the UPA government has come up with the Rural Employment Guarantee Programme which aims at providing a minimum days of employment to people living in the villages. This is a laudable programme, and if implemented sincerely it will provide employment to people during natural calamities like drought, floods, etc. The remedial measures for reducing unemployment may lay greater emphasis on creation of opportunities for self-employment, augmentation of productivity and income levels of the working poor, shift in emphasis from creation of the relief type of employment, to the building up of durable productive assets in the rural areas, and instead of attempting to revert somewhat to protectionist policies, the pace of privatisation will be accelerated.

8. THE GAME OF POLITICS

Politics is a game in the true spirit of the term. It has two or more parties contesting each other, each being equally dedicated to win. Each maintains a team, whether close knit or not, may be circumstantial, and has a lot at stake. Like any other game, not only the player takes interest but also a large audience to watch its every minute movement, cheer its wins and boo its losses. It has its own set of supporters, who may however be divided on their favourites from the team.

Any game requires a balance of mind or the physique or both, but politics requires both. One must have a sharp mind and should also be physically resilient enough to fight elections, do campaigns on a day and night basis, listen to a thousand voices at the same time and so on. Just as in any sport, the match or game may last for a short while, but the preparations go on for months. Practice makes a perfect sportsperson and so also practice makes a mature politician. Any sport lasts or is popular till people have interest in it, and politics scores very well on this front. People are addicted to politics and there is no drawing room where heated discussions over politics have not taken place. It is in acknowledgement of this fact that the media today focuses mainly on politics, relegating everything else to the background.

Politics and political thought has come a long way since and is no longer limited by states and territories alone; the politics of today has global implications and is of interest to both the intellectual and the common man. The wave of a general globalisation of things has not overlooked the most important aspect of man as a social being. In these times everything is global and local politics is invariably linked to world politics. The game of politics is played as passionately and meticulously in any part of the world. Theories do not alone suffice one to become a good politician. One has to live through the twist and turns of a political career. Maturity obviously comes with time. The real politician still continues though in a more subtle manner, but its vicious inclinations remain the same. Today's politician has less conscience and more greed for power as well as money and will go to any extent to reach his goals, even if he has to declare war and walk over the bodies of the thousands that die as a result.

Even today, it is self service of the mighty as it was centuries ago. Terminology has changed but basics remain the same. Hunger for power and control drives man in all the fields and will continue to do so into eternity, only the modus operandi will change. Politics was there and will continue to be there even if it turns from global to universal or to even inter-galactic. Just as man is a social animal, so also he is a political one. This game will go on, and with renewed vigour through the ages.

9. LEADERSHIP

Leadership has always been a key to my success in life. In today's business world, effective leadership at all levels is required. I use the same concepts in leading my family as I do in my business. Leadership does make a difference. I realize that without good physical health, today's leaders cannot stand up to the challenges of corporate life.

I have learned that weight does not matter, and the amount of body fat is countable but currently, am not disciplined in this area. I am convinced that lowering the amount of fat and increasing the lean muscle mass of my body, will help make me a better leader in today's corporate world. I must eat strategically to boost my business stamina, creativity and productivity. Currently, I do not eat strategically. I do not make time for a small, nutritious breakfast each day.

I have learned to better myself and must do this every day. Eating small meals like an apple after every two hours or so throughout the day keeps my energy up. I plan to tap into my body's survival instincts and force it to realise that it does not need to store fat against famine. I believe that my body will then operate at a higher metabolic rate and burn fat faster. I hope to build a pattern that will keep me fit and give me a total lifestyle change. I have learned from the six principles of anti-dieting that there will be backsliding. I hope to surround myself with the most positive people, who will encourage me to stay on track, as I will continue to encourage them. I have a problem with high stress levels now. I have learned that stress can be positive because it is energy expenditure in all its forms. I know that avoiding stress reverses functional capacity and seeking stress will help me reach my highest potential.

With the new knowledge I have gained from this class, I know that stress only becomes dangerous when it is not balanced by appropriate and adequate recovery. Calorie-counting will no longer be the way I diet. I will enjoy eating healthy foods because recovery means recapturing energy. Adequate sleep is at the top of my recovery list. Nutrition comes second, with the use of plenty of clean water to flush the toxins out of my body.

Exercise will provide an outlet for my stress, while allowing me to sweat the poisons out of my system. Exercise does improve my performance at work and with my family. I hope by using the concepts, I will be more energetic, effective, and creative. I have learned that I do need improvement in many areas of my life. Now I will begin working on improving myself. Guidance is something that everyone needs. I realise my immediate need for a suitable mentor. Over the years, my mentors have been rare. Through the concepts of remapping oneself, I have accomplished things such as financial security. A current weakness I am working on is finance. I appear to be somewhat of an extremist. I am dominant in most of my daily activities. I am working on listening to others more, thinking before I speak, while constantly observing my surroundings to improve myself. Wisdom is what I have learnt from my elders and the previous mentors I have mentioned. I am working on my sense of balance by learning to understand that various parts and principles of my education relate to each other in my life.

10. CORPORAL PUNISHMENT

Corporal Punishment is a way to punish misbehaving children in schools across the country. I believe that this is an extreme form of punishment for children. I believe this for a number of reasons.

A few of them are that children could get hurt, some parents don't want other adults hitting their children, and there are also better forms of punishment. In corporal punishment, children always run the risk of getting hurt. In some cases corporal punishment is not even necessary, because in cases where the offense is not very serious, then what is the purpose of getting the child physically harmed?

Then, on the other hand, if the offense is great enough for physical punishment to be enforced, then it should just be enforced to a certain extent. I believe that there is a fine line between punishment and abuse and this should be recognized in schools that still enforce corporal punishment.

Another reason that corporal punishment should be banned to a certain extent is because of the reason that some other parents do not want other adults harming kids in a physical way. Unless the parents give permission to do this at the beginning of the year, then I do not believe that the faculty of the school or any other adult has the right to lay hand on a particular child. I know that when I have kids I do not want anyone to lay hands on my kids except for me or my family. Another reason I do not entirely agree with corporal punishment is because of the fact that there are better forms of punishment that exist today.

For instance, say, that a child has gotten in trouble doing something, that child would be hurt more if something they adore were taken away from them for a certain period of time than to harm the child physically. This is a better form of punishment that would help them to learn responsibility and it will not harm the child in any fashion. These are a few good reasons as to why corporal punishment should be banned to a certain extent. There are many more effective ways to treat bad behaviour than by physical punishment and I think that we should look at these ways more carefully and consider them as an alternative to corporal punishment.

11. ROLE OF WOMEN IN CRIMINAL JUSTICE

Corrections have been a field dominated primarily by men. Women entering in this field have to struggle against the resistance presented while entering these types of jobs.

Criminal justice and women have been terms that have not been heavily associated. However, women do play a major role in the criminal justice system, whether they are the offenders, victims or criminal justice professionals. The role of women in criminal justice often depicts women as the victims in order to keep in place the ideologies of women being subordinate, feeble, and unable to take care of themselves against their aggressor.

Women are not only victimised but they also play roles of the offenders and criminal justice professionals, contrary to popular belief. Although women have made strives to progress, they still represent the lowest line of sworn in officers. Women are very versatile in their involvement with the criminal justice system.

It is also important for us as a society to understand that women are major functionaries in the criminal justice system although their isn't an enormous amount of literature about it. Women are represented in every dimension of the criminal justice system. The depictions of women in the media are influential factors for women who have chosen this male-dominated workforce. The traditional roles of women being housewives and mothers have in some ways hindered the process of them becoming a dominant workforce in the field of corrections.

A woman saving a man would challenge our societal ideologies of women being weak and feeble. I had a discussion with three women officers, they were all troopers and one was even a captain, and this article really elaborates on the discussion that I had with these women. The article really got into the nuts and bolts of women as criminal justice professionals, and it also was very informative when it discussed the hierarchical role of women as police officers; these women whom I spoke to were very clear about the harassment and isolation on the job.

The portrayal of women as not being able to do the job is a justification of treating women so poorly on the job, when the sad truth in many instances is that their male counterparts want them to fail in order to assert their male dominance. Women police officers in theory have the same protections as their male counterparts; however, this is a claim that can be disputed. Women do not have the protection against their images that are presented in the media and the images that make women more likely to be taken for granted by society at large.

12. WELL-ROUNDED EDUCATION

The first day of class for a college student is like drawing cards in a poker game. Just as the cards that one receives determine their outcome in poker, the types of professors a student gets on the first day will determine the success of their year.

The difference between helpful and harmful professors can easily result in a much lower grade. College professors have a wide range of personalities and backgrounds. However, professors fall into one of these three categories: helpful, malicious, and uncaring. One type of professor in the college system is the helpful professor.

These professors can be recognised right away by their smile and joyfulness in the classroom. These professors give upbeat and interesting lectures, and are always looking for the classes input to make sure they comprehend. These professors are always willing to chat with students, whether after the class or during office hours; the helpful professor will always take time out to talk with students about the given subject, college matters, or even problems of life that do not even have a bearing on the subject. Tests in the helpful professor's class are never difficult if one know the subject matter. The professor understands how stressful testing can be and is only interested in seeing whether or not the student has grasped the facts presented to them. Good students receive good marks in the helpful professor's class. Those professors appreciate hard work and duly reward it. The best kind of teacher to get that first day is the helpful professor.

The second type of professor one can get is the malicious professor. These professors have a sour attitude towards life in general; therefore, they want the students to be miserable as well. Their lectures are never to the point and usually stray off to make some negative point about life. They encourage students to ask questions, but only so that they can make the person with the question feel incompetent for asking it. They are willing to talk with a student after the class, but unlike the helpful professor, the malicious professors are only there to criticise. They will emphasise the student's faults but never point out their strengths, thus lowering the self-esteem of the student.

The tests given by the malicious professors are

vague, full of trickery, and composed of the most difficult material. These tests are not designed to survey the student's knowledge of the subject, but rather to trip them up and make them fail. If one works really hard it is possible to earn good marks in this type of professor's class, but in general the marks will be as low as the malicious professor can make them.

The third type of professor is the uncaring professor. These types of instructors have lost interest in teaching; therefore, they do not put any effort into it. These professors can be recognised by their monotonous tone of voice and lack of interest in the subject.. This type of instructor is reluctant to give out in office hours and can hardly ever be found there.

The personality of the professor makes up as much of its content as does the subject matter. Therefore, it is important when choosing a course to find out what type of teacher is instructing the class: helpful, malicious or uncaring.

13. GLOBAL WARMING

What happens when too much carbon dioxide gets admitted into the Earth's atmosphere? The condition known as Global Warming occurs. Global warming is the rising of the Earth's surface temperature due to chemicals in the atmosphere. Global warming has many threats on the climate and even the health of the people on this planet.

The first thing I think I should discuss while talking about global warming is, what causes it to occur. Gases such as carbon dioxide, methane and nitrous oxide, which are known as greenhouse gases, all build up in the atmosphere of the Earth. All these gases make it so that it becomes harder for the radiation that the sun shines into the atmosphere to escape. The heat continues to build up and this is what causes the temperatures to increase.

Global warming also helps the Earth and it has been for many years. Without global warming, the Earth's temperature would be a lot lower than the 60-degree average. Unfortunately, due to many harmful 'greenhouse gases' being placed into the atmosphere, instead of the temperature staying at a constant, keeps rising. On the islands usually where native tribes live, if the sea level rises three fourths of a metre, then half of the islands will sink. This could happen in many different islands around the world and if the water keeps on rising as it is, then the farming land near the seashore will be flooded and the crops will be destroyed, and many farmers will be left without much to live off?

The melting of the glaciers is also causing some problems in the Himalayas. Many of the tips of the mountain are in that area. Massive flooding and rivers that are well above their normal levels are threatening the crops and homes in the area. Many of the locals that live in the area and scientists that are surveying the area are saying that the glaciers are melting at a phenomenal rate. Another danger that comes with the changing of the climate is the increased heat which causes more evaporation to occur in the hotter climates.

There will be more precipitation in many other climates that are not used to handling massive rainfalls. Increased rainfall also leads to the speeding up of the process of the sea levels rising. Health is also something that gets threatened because of global warming. Heat becomes a huge factor in the health of humans, especially the elders. Incidents such as heat stroke, head's exhaustion and other diseases increase drastically. The heat makes it possible for mosquitoes and other insects to transmit diseases.

14. PRESERVATION OF WILD LIFE

Man's ever increasing needs and greed has led him to intrude indiscriminately into the world of nature. He has not only lost the awe and fear which was a part of nature-worship in the early religions, but has developed an almost ruthless attitude towards the world of animals. He has felled trees, built dams and disturbed the peaceful seclusion of the forests. With thousands of men working on dam sites and vehicular traffic moving round the clock, animals are forced to retreat further into the fast receding forests. Added to these, the rapid industrialization with its accompanying pollution, the use of pesticides and insecticides has made the struggle for survival a losing battle for large numbers of birds and animals.

Nuclear explosions and even holiday picnickers are driving the fish towards extinction. The lack of oxygen in the coastal waters drives them to their death. Another contributory factor is man's desire to capture animals and keep them in captivity. The idea is not wrong but the unimaginative method is wrong. For lack of space, animals are kept in small, uniform cages, without bothering to cater to their individual needs and living habits. In order to avoid cluttering of their cages they are provided with the necessary perches, branches or wooden trunks which they can bore into. They are thus frustrated, unhappy and at times unduly ferocious. Yet animals and birds are necessary, man needs them first of all to retain the balance in the world of nature: and also to keep a part of himself alive for the tenderness which birds and animals arouse is perhaps the most unselfish emotion.

Preservation of wild life means preventing the extinction of species no matter how ungainly or unattractive they may be. The disposal of solid wastes into sea waters should be checked and controlled regularly. If nuclear experiments have to be conducted they should be done on a very limited scale and only in selected sites.

In many countries the old fashioned concept of a zoo has changed and more imagination is brought into play. As far as possible, conditions most conducive to their growth are created and there is an attempt to cater to the varying individual needs of the animals. And this is as it should be. Animals need their natural habitat in order to flourish. Wide spaces, ponds and pools provide them this. More and more specialised zoos are coming into being. Those animals which cannot procreate in captivity are being gradually allowed to return to wild life. The worst enemy of animals is man with his superior intelligence and ability to use machines and medicines to help him.

It's man's hunting instinct and his desire to exercise powers which have led him into this inconsiderate attitude towards animals. Many countries have attempted to curb this by proclaiming various birds and animals either as national animals or as protected animals and by imposing a ban on the shooting of these animals. All these measures are not enough to help preserve wild life. More than these, what is required is to check man's attitude towards animals. Man thinks of them as raw material for consumption and not as fellow beings. What had helped preserve nature in the past was the attitude of divinity towards them. Today, if we cannot have a divine feeling, we can at least cultivate an anthropomorphic attitude.

15. POPULATION CONTROL

Now a days with our current technology the increases in disease outbreak and famine is not much of a factor any more. War is not considered a valid population control method due to today's "new" wars. Without the three largest population controllers much of a factor any more, population is free to run out of control.

This provides us with an ever-increasing controversy: whether government or society should dictate family size. I believe that society can infringe indirect controls over family size, but these are considered more community norms as opposed to hard fast rules such as the governments can set.

First of all, it is a natural and religious right to produce offspring. Breed multiply and populate has been the belief since the beginning of time. The idea is to grow population so that our beliefs and the way of life may spread and be passed on. Who is then government to take these right away?

Governmental control over family size goes against everything that the society stands for. This would be an age-old idea called 'freedom'. When a government starts dictating the kind and size of family a person can have, till then almost all freedom is lost. Another topic briefly addressed above is the aborting and murdering of babies that aren't male.

A first hand example of this is China. China regulates or gives incentives to families that only produce one child. This is where the problem begins because most families want this child to be male. Male children are the providers and will go out and join the working world. They will be "successful". Many female babies are aborted once their sex is determined. If sex is not determined before birth, once born many, female babies are abandoned or destroyed. This shows cruelty that government-controlled family size will push people to destroy them. Government should control family size because in most instances, the general population cannot handle this for themselves.

A prime example of this is our already over-crowded inner cities. People with chemical addictions and no financial means, are cracking out babies right and left. They have no means of providing for all of these children. Government currently provides for these under-privileged children, that as cruel as it sounds, should not have been born.

I have a first hand example of this problem. A family friend in another state has adopted three crack babies from the same mother; this mother is also on welfare. This certain mother is by no means an exception. China is another example of why government needs to control population. Look at the current problems that they are faced with, because in earlier years they have done nothing. Left uncontrolled, the population will snowball out of control. The government needs to be aware of the ever-increasing population growth problem.

16. SOME CHANGES IN THE EDUCATIONAL SYSTEM

Education is to draw the best in children and to develop their faculties. Education is a complicated affair as it is supposed to equip children for life. Since life-styles are always changing the contents of education, it must also be changed accordingly. The school is supposed to provide the necessary experience to the child. When a child leaves the school he has to lead a useful life.

But in the traditional school, the child was supposed to learn mainly the 3 R's. So the chalk, board and the text books were the mainstay of the teacher who was to shape the character of the child. Rote memory was insisted upon and examinations were based on this learning technique. There was not much difference from year to year on the way children were tested. The examinations conducted did not test all the faculties of the child. So it was necessary for those who got through examinations to be trained afterwards. In short, children were very rarely taught to learn for themselves. This had continued for so long and the practice had to be abolished.

Once this was realised many new methods of teaching were tried and many new aids had been used for better education of children. Today, the school is a very complicated organisation and the teacher is no longer the sole arbiter. The children instead of being passive listeners, have been made active participants. They are handling, feeling, planning, creating and learning with newer tools and aids that the subjectivity has given place to healthy objectivity.

In order to make education relevant and meaningful, children are exposed to almost lifelike situations. They must know how to live as good citizens and honest members of society. The way the school creates situations with these ends in view is important. The ideal school must be run as a republic, the headmaster or the principal may preside over the republic, the lecturers serving as counsellors and, the students being the citizens.

On the intellectual side, the library and the laboratory must play a vital role. They complement and supplement more and more and the use of the library and the laboratory must be encouraged through proper assignments. The playing field, the various camps, the many organisations like the Red Cross, Scouting, NCC, NSS etc. have to be fully utilized to shape the character of the child. Beside the text books, there are other aids for learning. They must be judiciously used. In fact, there are hundreds of ways in which the audio-visual aids can be used with advantage.

Examinations should not be used to show the weakness but must be a yardstick for proving the all-round education of the student. The questions must be objective and reliable. The examinations must be welcomed by the students. In order to satisfy the diverse population, there must be diversity in programmes, approaches, resources, aims and room for experiment. Examinations should be a challenge for students.

The world is shrinking and nobody can feel parochial, so education must equip students for world understanding and world citizenry. Science and technology must find their place in every scheme of education. Every system of education must help turn out a fully developed and all-rounded personality.

17. SCHOOL VIOLENCE

Violence in schools is a great concern in our society. The concern is highlighted by the abundance of media coverage on a number of recent school shootings. With all of the news clips, sound bites, and Internet coverage swirling around in our heads, one might conclude that children are more violent today than they were in recent years.

But, school violence is not a new issue for the developed countries. School violence has been increasing day-by-day in the past, it was more an issue of juvenile delinquency than violent behaviour. The difference between the two generations is that today student conflicts are more likely to be solved with the use of weapons. The fact is that the gun is much more intimidating than a fist. There is nothing scarier than arriving at the school, afraid of what may happen next. Many students are faced with this problem everyday.

Children should feel safe when they walk into the school. Many people use violence as an expression to release feelings of anger or frustration. They think there are no answers to their problems and turn to violence to express their out of control emotions.

Others use manipulation as a way to control others or get something they want.

Violence is a learned behaviour. Like all learned behaviours, it can be changed. This isn't easy, though. Since there is no single cause of violence, there is no one simple solution. The best you can do is to learn to recognise the warning signs of violence, and to get help when you see them in your friends or yourself. Teachers tend to believe that school violence is a result of sociological factors such as lack of parental supervision, lack of family involvement and exposure to violence in the mass media. These factors could be traced to high divorce rates, both parents working, and the high availability of mass media, e.g., television, Internet, etc.

Students who live in fear of violence, witness violent acts, or become victims of violence, suffer an array of short-term and long-term consequences emotionally and physically. They have been found to be at greater risk for low school performance, absenteeism, truancy, school dropout and delinquency. In fact, research has shown that juveniles who are victimised, or who repeatedly witness violence, and do not receive immediate support in understanding and dealing with it, are at higher risk of using violence as a means of dealing with their own conflicts; thus repeating the cycle of violence.

Schools are not doing enough to protect students and other school personnel. Curing social ills could take a long time, so I propose a high security approach to the problem. The community may find this expensive and students oppressive, but how many more people should keep dying? I propose the following strategy: police officers in every school; metal detectors at each doorway; some type of dress code banning "big clothes" where weapons can be hidden; hall monitors in hallways, doorways, restrooms and cafeterias; preparing certain school personnel in weapon usage.

Allow them to carry and store weapons on the campus. If students knew someone else on campus had a gun to protect students, they may think twice about bringing one to school. This may sound severe, but this is a direct approach to the problem. Additional discipline is needed in order to stop school violence. We need more discipline in the family, in school, and even in public. We need to educate children that their actions do have consequences. As some countries, moral keeps declining and the murder rate continues to rise in schools, we will still be blaming our problems on anything but ourselves.

18. PROBLEMS WITH SOCIETY

There are many problems right now in the society. Some of these problems can be easily solved, or they can be impossible to solve depending upon how bad they are. Many people think these problems should be solved by the governments, since they are in charge. But we can also solve these problems if we get together. Though not all the problems, but some can certainly be solved.

I think the three major problems in the society today are: unemployment, violence, and pollution. The first problem in the society right now is unemployment. Many people today are either unemployed or underemployed. Some of these people just stay home and some time they would go out and try to get a job. If there are more people like this, the country would be poor and therefore the government will have to collect more taxes. Also the standard of living would decrease because of their income that is below the average income. Right now, there is also a big gap between the low-income people and the high-income people and this is becoming a great problem. Low-income people are starting to get lower wages and higher income people are starting to get higher wages.

Another problem in the society is violence. Today, there is much violence in the streets, some schools, and also in the media. This violence in the streets can cause the neighbourhood to become a bad place to live. This will cause people not to go there or move to other places because of this violence. There are also much violence and gangs in some schools, causing some of the schools to be very unsafe to go. With this violence and gangs, students will probably be afraid of these people. The media can contain violence. Their scenes of violence can cause kids to do whatever they see on the TV.

For example, my little brother likes to watch wrestling and he sometimes does wrestling and moves on to me for no reason, just thinking it's fun. Even though it doesn't hurt me because I'm bigger than him, he might hurt someone smaller in school or somewhere else.

The third problem in the society today is pollution. Many things these days cause pollution, such as cars, air conditioners, refrigerators, factories, etc. All these things together can cause a pollution problem in the society today. Refrigerators and air conditioners are also a problem to the ozone in the atmosphere because of the liquid called freon. These machines use this liquid to make it cold, but when these liquids are released from the machine, they release a gas that breaks down the ozone layers. In addition, cars can also cause a lot of pollution because of the carbon monoxide they produce. This would cause the air to go bad, cause global warming, which would cause the earth to have longer summers or longer winters, and would also cause acid rain.

In conclusion, unemployment, violence, and pollution should be considered to be the three major problems in the society today. People and the government should get together and try to solve these problems in order to make this planet a safe and good place to live. If these problems are not solved, there might not be an Earth in the future to live on.

19. THE LOSS OF INNOCENCE

Innocence is such a precious gift. A child doesn't know any better during the stage of innocence and is unable to reasonably distinguish the differences between right and wrong.

Children are blind towards the race and ethnicity of others. A kid will hang out with another kid no matter what; it is the lack of innocence and the ignorance we learn from adults that manipulate children otherwise. As adults, people have very little time to do things that they enjoy.

The adventurous mind is lost in time with the responsibilities that are bestowed upon adults. As adults people have more freedom to visit places and to do certain things, making it easier to do the thing, which they wanted to do during childhood but could not do. They do, however, feel that the lack of organisation and mental capacity of those without innocence would have a tremendously devastating impact on society in general. With the ongoing life of innocence, a large portion of individuals would never have the urge to learn, work, and act upon the necessary needs for humanity to survive. Without a proper education which is usually provided by those who no longer live in a world of innocence, people would not have the mental abilities to get a good job in life, thus providing little income for families and hurting the lives of children.

The lack of a good education and career would also harm the economy. Society would then take on a state much like communism. With the lack of hatred and worries that people have as children, people would feel that work is simply something they need to do to raise money. As long as innocence is kept alive, no one would be terribly angered at the lack of effort people put out in the workplace, resulting in a strong decline in production and quality of needed goods.

Although it seems as if decisions and events made during a person's childhood are totally irrelevant towards the rest of his/her life, these factors make a tremendous impact on the type of adult a person becomes. Another way of keeping innocence alive that would benefit humanity is the constant craving for fun and adventure. May be Hodlen Caufeild was wrong in wanting to save innocence. Perhaps innocence was meant to be lost.

There are certain things in life that probably should not be toyed around with. It was god's will to make things the way they are, and I am sure God has a good purpose for everything. All that remains to be said about innocence is to enjoy it before it lasts. It is certainly the happiest time of anyone's life.

20. SCHOOL PRIVATISATION

Our society, as a whole, has been heading towards a decentralised system of conducting its affairs. Large corporations have been getting larger, meanwhile, governments have been giving up increasing amounts of their control. This decentralisation has affected even former mainstays of government control, such as phone and power companies. As decentralisation becomes more of a reality, there has been a great deal of debate over what controls the government should maintain or relinquish.

The public school system has long been a source of frustration. Many feel the schools would run more efficiently and with better results if privately run companies were to take over. They feel that with the existing large, encumbering bureaucracy, the government is simply unable to provide the proper base that is necessary to support a successful school system. The proponents of privatised school systems have long maintained that governments are not as knowledgeable about individual school environments as themselves, and they have to manage many schools, whereas the owners of a specific private subsidised school would be well informed about the school's circumstances and can concentrate on that school alone. They say that the government's role should become that of regulator, not of schoolmaster, and since the private schools do not face the political constraints that the municipal governments face, they would be more able to adapt to change.

Since the operation of public schools is more bureaucratic and centralized than private subsidised schools, it is expected to inhibit rather than promote educational innovation. Private schools, being less bureaucratic and more decentralised, are expected to be more efficient organisations and to have a better perspective than their public school counterparts. They are also expected to provide a greater incentive and opportunity to come up with more innovative programmes than public schools do in order to stay competitive.

Bureaucracy is expected to hinder initiative and efficiency, whereas the private sector in general is expected to be more dynamic and responsive because of their need to stay competitive. It is hoped that this competitiveness will foster innovation. On the other side of the debate is the group that favours continued government control over the school system. They argue that privatising the schools would lead to a decreased focus on the needs of children with an increased emphasis placed on the bottom line. They maintain that the companies taking over for the government would focus their attention more on cutting corners to make larger profits rather than on the education of children.

With continued government control over the school system, there will remain a stability that is necessary to ensure a full and equal educational opportunity for all. Having the education system privatised would create inequalities in the method that education would be provided. Those who oppose privatisation agree that not only would municipal control maintain stability, but would also ensure fair and equal treatment for all. The same would not hold true if the schools were placed in private hands. Schools that do not make a profit along with teachers that are no longer needed would simply let go in order to save money or maintain profits. I can see that there are several benefits on both sides. The economic benefits are obviously in favour of a decentralised school structure.

21. PHYSICAL EDUCATION IN SCHOOLS

I believe that physical education in school is an essential curriculum for the development of all children. Early physical education classes provide children with a medium for progression from the random play stage to the eventual organised game and eventual structured learning.

Throughout this process, children learn the value of group dynamics. Values such as sharing, team-play, communication and respect for others become common practice. Apart from group development, physical education at an early age can also dramatically help children succeed in the classroom environment. All children learn at different rates. Learning new ideas and developing them in require time and much practice before reaching some success.

Most children at some point during this period will struggle. Physical education at this age can provide children with the opportunity to success and be a sort of mental recess. Games and play can be developed so that kids can associate learning with activity. Since kids enjoy games and play and can easily succeed in this medium, therefore, physical activity will bumper confidence that will last forever in every child. Success in play can be carried over into the classroom and in future life endeavours. Physical education for children is also very important in the development of their bodies. During this early period in their lives, children can develop poor eating habits that make physical play difficult to participate in, eventually weaning children away from physical activity participation. It is therefore important to keep kids involved in physical participation, teaching them the values of participation, thereby setting the foundation for physical participation for the rest of their lives.

Apart from the physical rewards of physical education, children can also expand their creative minds in physical play. Through play, children are free to be as creative as they wish.

Experimentation of the mind and body is a regular occurrence in playgrounds as kids adapt games and develop new challenges for their minds and body. Playgrounds are transformed into foreign lands to explore, fields become stadiums, backyard rinks become professional hockey coleseums where legends are made and anyone can score the winning goal and race to victory. These are just some of the values that early physical education can provide to a developing child. The importance of these values as developed through physical education, I feel, will dictate the levels of personal success any individual will have in their life.

22. CAPITAL PUNISHMENT

Capital punishment is a brutal and antiquated concept that must be abolished in the name of civilised society. A humane culture cannot abide by the organised extermination of human beings in the name of justice. In the United States, dozens of people are put to death every year like stray animals, only perhaps in less humane ways. The methods of capital punishment vary greatly, but none are publicly accepted as humane.

Society's support for the death penalty is waning, but there is still enough support in the United States to keep it legal in many states. The death penalty exercises only the most primal instincts to kill and extract revenge in an organised fashion. This is why the death penalty must be abolished entirely: to allow society to function in a civilised manner in which every person has the right to live. Capital punishment is hypocritical, selection is arbitrary and biased, and the practice itself is cruel and inhumane. By allowing the organised extermination of living human beings the government is telling the public that they have the right to extinguish anyone they think is a murderer.

The idea of killing another is inherently hypocritical. By enforcing capital punishment, the government is telling the public that it is okay to kill as long as you have more power than the person you are killing. This is of course a very cut-and-dried interpretation, but it is what the message boils down to. The problem with such a hypocritical notion as an eye for the eye, is its fundamental inconsistency.

In order to practice what they preach, the courts would have to find a way to steal from thieves, betray traitors, and rape rapists. This is obviously ludicrous. Besides the central hypocrisies and inconsistencies of the punishment itself, the selection of those subjected to it is also unfair and prejudiced. Race, social status, economic status, level of education, and location of crime are key in the selection of those to be executed. Of course, one may think it is good that such a relatively small number of people are executed, but this number represents the frivolous inclination of the legal system.

In fact, since the reinstatement of the death penalty in the United States in 1976, only five white persons have been executed for killing a black person. This informs public that the value of their lives depends on their race and the jury's opinion of them. This sets back years of struggle for civil rights in North America. Society suffers in the face of such things and pre-dispose 'justice'. Besides being arbitrary in selection, once selected, the condemned must undergo a series of cruel and torturous events.

The enforcement of capital punishment is a sadistic and macabre activity which appeals to the more grim aspects of human nature: wrath and malice. The condemned is told of his execution date and is then confined in a maximum security prison to await his execution. This is hardly a fitting punishment even if one believes that death is the answer. For there to be an equivalence between criminal homicide and execution, Albert Camus wrote, the death penalty would have to punish a criminal who had warned his victim of the date at which he would inflict a horrible death on him, and who from that moment onward had confined him at his mercy for months. Such a monster is not encountered in private life. The fact that society feels such abhorrence for murders is veritably human, but exactly to the criminal what caused them to hate the criminal in the first place, is ridiculous.

23. CHILD LABOUR AND SOCIETY

The concern of child labour exists from poverty. We have to understand as why children go to work. If parents don't send their children to work I am sure factories will not be able to consume them. The dream of education to children is impossible unless suitable employment opportunities are made available to at least one person in the family. Simply by opening schools and providing books are not sufficient measures. We need to understand the reason behind child labour, that is poverty and unemployment. Minimising poverty and creation of more and more suitable jobs to parents are the only solution of the eradication of the majority of child labour problem.

Some percentage of child labour comes from brutality/harassments by parents or step parents. They are mainly from urban areas of lower middle-income groups. This percentage is too little and easily controllable by penalties to such parents and children's rights. But rural poverty and lack of employment or partial employment and illiteracy has given birth to a majority of child labour problems. Our understanding should be a little more practical as no parents want their children to work at the age when children are to study and play. The system of child labour prevails in the countries which are poor or underdeveloped.

Education of fewer children to become citizens is a soft method of controlling, but is useful to only the literate class who are already adapted to fewer children. Semi-literates with partial success and Illiterates have their reasons - religion is one of the big factors that illiterates misunderstand. Religious leaders are very helpful; taking religious leaders into confidence would definitely give partial success. The second reason what the illiterates perceive is, that the more the children more, the income and this perception is definitely wrong and dangerous. For this some harsh steps are to be taken.

Announcing incentives and disincentives to have limited children will be high success to control excessive growth of population, and also entitlement of subsidised food articles and services. It looks difficult in democratic countries; subsidy to be allocated by grading small family and big family would help. Entitlement of government positions and promotions. Entitlement of special preference for small family of poor category to upgrade standard of living by way of loan and education of small scale industry to set up. Accountability of Central and State heads: Each central/ state/ district and local area head should be made responsible and accountable in his or her legislative area by mutual agreement.

Discouraging over population is rather killing the world. Lack of education in these countries is the main reason. The NGOs should come with ideas to encourage countries to introduce incentives and disincentives for a smaller family.

There should be joint effort by international societies and local governments to reform and minimize poverty and bring social security in unorganised sectors and curtail excessive growth of population. World's biggest enemy is excessive population. These play important roles in uplifting child labour.

24. THE IMPACT OF COMPUTERS

The computer technology has solved many problems but it also has created some, including a certain amount of culture shock as individuals attempt to deal with the new technology. A major role of computer science has been to alleviate such problems, mainly by making computer systems cheaper, faster, more reliable and easier to use. Computers are for ever present in the workplace. Word processors and computer software packages that simplify the creational and the modification of documents have largely replaced the typewriter.

Electronic mail has made it easier to send messages worldwide via computer communication networks. Office automation has become the term for linking workstations, printers, database system, and other tools by means of a local area network. An eventual goal of office automation has been termed as "paperless office." Although such changes ultimately make office work much more efficient, they have not been without cost in terms of purchasing and frequently upgrading the necessary hardware and software and of training workers to use the new technology. Computer-integrated manufacturing is a relatively new technology arising from the application of many computer science subdisciplines to support the manufacturing enterprise.

In short, Computer Integrated Manufacturing has the potential to enable manufacturers to build cheaper, higher quality products and thus improve their competitiveness.

Making a telephone call no longer should conjure up visions of operators connecting cables by hand or even of electrical signals causing relays to click into place and effect connections during dialing. The telephone system now is just a multilevel computer network with software switches in the network nodes to route calls get through much more quickly and reliably than they did in the past.

A disadvantage is the potential for dramatic and widespread failures; for as has happened and the downside of this technology is the potential for security problems. Intruders can see packets travelling on a network and can perhaps interpret them to obtain confidential information. Computer technology had a significant impact on retail stores but the smallest shops have replaced the old-fashioned cash register with a terminal linked to a computer system.

The terminal may require that the clerk type in the code for the item; but more and more frequently the checkout counter include a bar-code scanner, a device that directly reads into the computer the UPC printed on each package. Cash-register receipts can then include brief descriptions of the items purchased, and the purchase information is also relayed back to the computer to cause and immediate adjustment in the inventory data. The inventory system can easily alert the manager when the supply of some item drops below a specified threshold. In the case of retail chains linked by networks, the order for a new supply of an item may be automatically generated and sent electronically to the supply warehouse.

Although increased reliability has been achieved by implementing such computerisation, a drawback is that only automotive repair shops with a large investment in high-tech interfaces and diagnostic tools for these computerised systems can handle any but the simplest repairs.

25. MEDIA VIOLENCE AND ITS EFFECTS ON CHILDREN

Children everywhere are being born into a world of images and messages, which are largely separated from their home, school and spiritual lives. In today's society, storytellers are seldom parents, grandparents, teachers or the clergy; instead they are a handful of distant forces with something to sell. The unique thing about the media industry is that in global and corporate domination they have become part of our culture as well as our identity.

Social scientists and child advocates have been exploring the effects of media for decades, yet it is recently that the concern has generated as public debate. Historical disagreements concerning the effect of violence revealed in works of art and entertainment have resonated over the centuries. We must ask ourselves whether or not our versions of entertainment exhibits any more violence than the past forms of recreation, for example, gladiatorial games or public hangings.

People during all periods of time have derived some sort of sensual, aesthetic and even at time erotic thrills from viewing a violent act. It would be unfair to conclude that in today's society such spectators and consumers of media are guided by no other motive. Extreme acts have happened in recent history; though there has always been crime and violence, never have there been such extreme acts, as the few which have been committed in recent years.

As technology improves and the amount of violent entertainment increases, images are becoming more graphic and result in a more realistic portray of violence. Television viewing affects children of different ages in different ways. While children may spend many hours in front of a television set at an early age, the programming has little effect. At the age of two a child will imitate the actions of a live model, and the example of a parent more than of a model on television. However, by the age of three the child will begin to imitate the T.V. characters. The attitudes toward television drastically change over a child's life. While researching the effects of television, various points need to be taken into consideration. Certain issues effect people in different ways, for example, pornography. However, most parents do not realise that whether aggression is presented in a realistic way or in a cartoon, it makes no difference to a child who has a difficult time differentiating between the two. Exposure to violence is not believed to increase aggression, but being aggressive increases preference for violent television. Children observe what is considered novel aggressive behaviour and learn that vicariously aggressive acts are rewarded. The more the child can relate to the characters in the programme, the more likely they will be to emulate the characters, actions. Not only the actions of the child reflect the programmes viewed but watching a violent programme causes desensitisation.

26. EARTHQUAKE

An earthquake is the shaking of the earth's surface caused by rapid movement of the earth's rocky outer layer. The sudden shaking of the ground that occurs when masses of rock change position below the earth's surface is called an earthquake.

Earthquakes, called temblors by scientists, occur almost continuously. Fortunately, most of them can be detected only by sensitive instruments called seismographs. Others are felt as small tremors. Some of the rest, however, cause major catastrophes. They produce such tragic and dramatic effects as destroyed cities, broken dams, earth slides, giant sea waves called tsunamis, and volcanic eruptions.

A very great earthquake usually occurs at least once a year in some part of the world. Mankind has long been concerned about earthquake hazards. Thus, the violent shaking that accompanies many earthquakes often causes rockslides, snow avalanches, and landslides. In some areas these events are frequently more devastating than the earth tremor itself. Floods and fires are also caused by earthquakes.

Floods arise from tsunamis along coast lines, from large-scale seiches in enclosed bodies of water such as lakes and canals, and from the failure of dams. Fire produced the greatest property loss following the 1906 San Francisco earthquake, when 521 blocks in the city centre burned uncontrollably for three days.

Fire also followed the 1923 Tokyo earthquake, causing much damage and hardship for the citizens. Causes most of the worst earthquakes are associated with changes in the shape of the earth's outermost shell, particularly the crust. These so called tectonic earthquakes are generated by the rapid release of strain energy that is stored within the rocks of the crust, which on continents is about 22 miles thick. A small proportion of earthquakes is associated with human activity.

Dynamite or atomic explosions, for example, can sometimes cause mild quakes. The injection of liquid wastes deep into the earth and the pressures resulting from holding vast amounts of water in reservoirs behind large dams can also trigger minor earthquakes. The strongest and most destructive quakes, however, are associated with ruptures of the earth's crust, which are known as faults. Although faults are present in most regions of the world, earthquakes are not associated with all of them. Pressures from within the earth strain the great rock masses beneath the earth's surface. The strain builds until suddenly the masses move along the faults, thereby releasing energy. The masses slip and slide in opposite directions along this fracture in the rock, shaking the ground above. The masses may move up and down, sideways, or vertically and horizontally. On the earth's surface displacement of the ground may vary from several centimetres to many metres. Some fault lines appear on the surface of the earth. Shock waves shifting the rock in an earthquake causes waves called seismic waves to spread through the rock in all directions.

27. POVERTY

Poverty is a global problem, and it has existed from the beginning of civilisation. Hunger, homelessness, and lack of health care are major aspects of this worldwide dilemma. Many countries are in complete poverty and the majority is third-world countries.

Throughout the world, poverty has plagued all the countries. In smaller, under-developed countries many people die from starvation. These countries cannot afford to support their citizens. Due to their financial problems, the people lack proper shelter and clothing to keep themselves warm during the cold months. Since they lack adequate shelter and clothing, diseases occur all over. These diseases develop a lot easier with poor nutrition.

This perspective sees society offering plenty of opportunity to anyone able and willing to take advantage of it. The poor are whoever cannot or will not work, women and men with fewer skills, less schooling, and little motivation. Everyone does not have the same physical abilities and mental abilities. Poor health and abilities prevent some people from holding a job. Through science people have been able to hold on to jobs a lot easier.

It has increased the need for professional workers and lowered the demand for the unskilled. So, people with higher education will get paid higher income, and people with lower education will get paid lower income.

Simply creating jobs will not help eliminate poverty because there are some people who are disabled and just cannot work. The government social welfare programmes help to add income to many people. These people could be the retired, unemployed, disabled, or widowed. In order to help the less fortunate, the people that are employed are taxed to raise money to pay for social security and other benefits. For the higher income worker taxes are higher, and for lower income worker taxes are lower. Sadly enough, poverty has struck some countries.

A variety of things were done to lower the unemployment rate. One important thing is the big industry, like automation, computer, that came into the area. The government has been doing a lot to decrease unemployment. They have been creating more jobs for the people.

Poverty can happen in big countries like India and China. As old people today live longer their physical bodies are not able to work properly as demanded. I think that the most important thing for people and each country is to have a feeling trying to understand poverty and avoid it to happen as disaster. The first thing people need is to invest is education and knowledge. Job training is the main part to eliminate unemployment rate, and poverty. However, we cannot give it as the only excuse, because the world is changing rapidly, and disasters happen every year and everywhere in the world. Thus, helping people is the way to solve the problem.

28. SOCIAL IMPACT OF THE INTERNET

The advent of Internet communication technology is in and of itself, a positive move toward overall global advancement, but the costly social impact is what concerns families and the sociologists. The positive aspects of the Internet are many and there is almost nothing that cannot be accomplished from the comfort of one's own home: grocery shopping, buying merchandise, paying bills, researching for term papers and even striking up relationships with people half way across the world. Communication, which once consisted of putting pen to paper, has now been reduced to a few key strokes and click of a mouse; indeed, people are able to correspond via E-mail faster and easier than traditional mail services could ever hope to offer.

The positive aspects of the Internet are immeasurable and go without saying; this essay's focus is on the negative effects of the Internet. The social impact: alienation from institutions such as the family, education and places of work may result from the following factors: lack of face-to-face socialization is turning into a considerable problem for those who have locked themselves inside the anonymity of their computers. Indeed studies have shown the tendency for people to become significantly stressed, depressed and lonely with each hour spent in the obscure world of Internet chatting. There is proof to substantiate the claim that the longer people spend chatting on the Internet, the less sociable they become; a considerable amount of further research must be done to determine the extent of damage this has on society.

The Internet introduces an invasion of western culture into the homes of unsuspecting parents, which may lead to a loss of one's own culture and adopting a new foreign one. The adoption of a new culture will cause the general public to resist this change; thus the consequences will lead the youth to feel rejected and further amplify the already existing social problem of alienation from society as a whole.

I also get the shocking news about the Internet and its effects on our society–did you know that 85% of all pictures on the Internet are pornographic in nature? That makes me wonder what kind of exposure the youth are encountering, and what are the effects on their values. A recent report published on CNN.com states that more than 50 percent parents of children between 11 and 15 years say they allow their kids to go online whenever they feel like. The number increases to 75 percent for teenagers older than 16. This is a very serious matter and should be given careful and detailed thought.

29. HURRICANES

Hurricanes are nature's forces that exist every where. Hurricanes could be considered one of the most powerful of all these forces that can cause tremendous amounts of destruction. A hurricane is a powerful whirling storm of winds that measure 200-300 miles in diameter. Hurricanes are areas of low pressure that form over the oceans in tropical regions in either the north Atlantic Ocean or eastern north Pacific Ocean. In the west Pacific Ocean hurricanes are called typhoons, and in the Indian Ocean they are called Cyclones.

Hurricanes develop from easterly waves and these easterly waves are long narrow regions of low pressure that occur in ocean winds called trade winds. The waves may grow into a tropical depression, which are winds from 1 to 31 miles per hour. Then they can grow into a tropical storm, which are winds from 32 to 73 miles per hour. These waves then turn into what you call hurricanes and hurricanes are winds greater than 74 miles per hour.

The winds swirl around a portion of the storm called the eye. This is a calm area in the centre of the storm. It is about 20 miles in diameter and has little wind and clouds. The storm clouds that are around the eye of the storm are called wall clouds. Inside these wall clouds there are most of the heaviest rains and the strongest winds. Outside of wall clouds are clouds called rain clouds. They have winds and rain and make up most of the diameter of the storm but nothing as powerful as the wall clouds.

Hurricanes usually occur during the months of June to November and highly occur during the month of September. Eight hurricanes occur a year on average but 15 have occurred in one year's time in the Atlantic Ocean. In the Northern Hemisphere the winds of a hurricane move around the eye counter clockwise due to the gravitational pull from the North Pole. In the Southern Hemisphere the winds move around the eye clockwise.

The eye of the hurricane travels over land at an average of 10 to 15 miles per hour. The atmospheric disturbance that causes hurricanes start approximately in the latitudes between

5-30 degrees on both sides of the equator. Hurricanes start moving towards land picking speed, strength, and size. They will then drift away from the equator as they reach temperate latitude where they are called extra tropical and travel over the land bring havoc and destruction to all that they pass over. The winds and the rains over the sea along with the force of the sea produce huge waves called storm surge. These storm surges cause lots of flooding and damage to coastlines, especially if they happen at high tide. The storm weakens as it moves over land because hurricanes need the warm sea to supply energy to it through evaporation. Also the friction of the storm over the land causes the storm to slow down. Meteorologists of the National Weather Service keep a close watch over the Atlantic and Pacific oceans if there are any storms brewing. They collect such information as air pressure, temperature, and wind speeds.

Hurricanes are an act of nature and although they are attempted to be controlled, they can't really ever be changed. This is why nature is so amazing, making hurricanes is one of nature's most powerful weapons, even more amazing than the forests all the way.

30. SCIENCE IN DAILY LIFE

In the history of mankind, advent of Science is the greatest blessing. Science has come to relieve mankind from sufferings, ignorance and gives it the power to control nature. It has been defined as a systematised body of wisdom and knowledge which can give rise to greater inventions. Science has also been known as a faithful servant of man who serves all his life and as per the orders of man. Science can be harmful if we misuse it.

Science has brought about far-reaching changes in every sphere of our daily life. Now everybody can afford to avail the benefits of luxuries and comforts created by Science. Science has made goods cheaper and readily available and has brought them within reach of every individual. All kinds of gadgets of music, entertainment and communication have been brought to our door with the help of Science. Surely, the life of man is very different from what it used to be a few years back. Truly, Science has given ears to the deaf, eyes to the blind and limbs to the crippled.

In everyday life, we have to communicate with

different friends and relatives, various official people for general purposes and many people to be contacted at very far off distances. However, time and distance both have been conquered by Science. Whether we want to communicate or travel, both are possible within seconds. For communication, we have telephones, mobiles, wireless, E-mail, and internet, etc., for faster travelling, airplanes are being used. Railways have made journeys swift, safe and comfortable. The entire world has shrunk into a small family. Modern ships have conquered turbulent waters and are perfectly safe for travelling and transportation of goods.

Health is wealth. This has been made possible with modern machines. Science has invented ways to peep inside the human body to tackle diseases of human beings through X-ray machines. Diseases can easily be detected and various tests conducted within a few seconds. Complicated operations are possible and are successful with the help of equipments and machines invented with the help of Science. Human life would get transformed into new horizons and heights of prosperity when atomic energy is fully utilised for peaceful purposes.

A big contribution of Science in our daily life is electricity. Without electricity, there would have been complete darkness after evening hours and no industry could function without the power of electricity. We have been able to control the effects of weather change with electrical energy. All fans, coolers and air-conditioners in summer and all kinds of heating gadgets in winter, function with the help of electricity. Entertainment through cinema is one of the most remarkable inventions of science in our daily life. It provides us cheap and enjoyable pastime and comfort from tensions of daily life. Now each household has television and radios which are the fastest medium of mass communication made possible by Science.

In spite of Science as a blessing in our daily life, we remain in constant fear of mass destruction weapons invented by Science. Another disadvantage of Science has been the misuse of mass media for propaganda. Sometimes information stories and facts are blown out of proportion leading to tension among the masses. Much of communal tension within the country has been the creation of media. Mass media is used by anti-social elements to spread rumours and false information. Once a story is circulated, it spreads like a forest fire, thanks to mass media. It is certainly up to mankind to utilize the benefits of Science for welfare of all or to indulge in making mass destruction weapons for miseries of future generations. Science can further be utilized to make our daily life more prosperous, comfortable and full of happiness.

31. THE POPULATION GROWTH RATE IN INDIA

Concern over Population Growth Rate in India for many years has been voiced over the seemingly unchecked rate of population growth in India, but the most recent indications are that some success is being achieved in slowing the rate of population growth. The progress which has been achieved till date is still only of a modest nature and should not serve as a premature cause for complacency. Moreover, slowing of the rate of population growth is not incompatible with dangerous population increase in a country like India which has so huge a population base to begin with. Nevertheless, the most recent signs do offer some occasion for adopting as certain degree of cautious optimism in regard to the problem. One important factor which is responsible for viewing the future with more optimism than may previously have been the case of increase in the size of the middle class, a tendency which has been promoted by the current tendency to ease restrictions on entrepreneurship and private investment.

It is a well-known fact that as persons become

more prosperous and better educated, they begin to undertake measures designed to eliminate the size of their families. Ironically, the state of Kerala which had a Communist-led government for many years represented a population planning model because of its implementation of programmes fostering education and the emancipation of women. The success of such programmes has indicated that even the poorer classes can be induced to think in terms of population control and family planning through education, but increased affluence correspondingly increases the pressure for the limitation of family size, for parents who enjoy good life, want to pass it on to their children under circumstances where there will be enough to go around. In contrast, under conditions of severe impoverishment, there is not only lack of knowledge of family planning or access to modes of birth control, but children themselves are likely to be viewed as an asset. Or, perhaps one might more accurately say with regard to India, sons are viewed as an asset.

Under conditions of severe impoverishment, attended as it has traditionally been by high childhood mortality rates, it has been estimated for India that in order to have a 95 per cent probability of raising a son to adulthood, the couple should have at least six children. In general, direct efforts on the part of government to promote family planning has only limited success in India. In large part this has been due to the factors which have traditionally operated in Indian culture and society to promote large families. It might be noted that the most common family planning modes have proven difficult to implement under Indian conditions.

Where government efforts are concerned, for mass consumption only these methods are advocated : sterilization and condoms. Sterilization has traditionally met with strong resistance among uneducated sectors of the population who associate it with loss of virility or femininity, and, often being irrevocable, it has been a source of understandable concern in a society where couples who may already have several children risk losing some or all of them as a result of such factors as epidemics, earthquakes or floods. In addition to the elimination of girl babies, either through outright murder or denying them food and care traditionally given to boys, abortion, on the basis of amniocentesis, has been another means of population control where girl babies are concerned.

32. ABANDONED – OUR MORAL DUTIES

Morality is essential for the future of a civilisation. Morality includes such values as honesty, the pursuit of truth, responsibility, duty, fairness in interpersonal relations, concern for one's immediate neighbours, respect for property, loyalty and duty to one's spouse and children, the work ethic and keeping one's word. The emphasis is upon the duty and responsibility of the individual. No society can function efficiently or humanely and no civilisation can endure without these values. The failure to assume responsibility for one's actions and the tendency to look to government for everything are among the consequences of the breakdown of traditional morality.

Traditional morality is inestimably important. The abandonment of traditional morality leads to expropriation of private property, heavy taxation, theft, waste, compulsory association, totalitarian thought control, sexual exploitation, homeless children, fraud and dishonesty, disloyalty to family, ever increasing government power and control, envy, indiscipline, laziness, individual irresponsibility, indecency, rudeness, impoliteness, social engineering, genocide and not to mention, impiety.

Destroy a society's values and you can manipulate the people. The values of a society derive over its spiritual and moral foundations. When those foundations are destroyed, a vacuum is created and people can be manipulated according to the ideology and power ambitions of ruling elites. All religions emphasise the importance of duties and responsibilities as distinct from rights. The Ten Commandments are duties. There is an emphasis on rights to the near exclusion of duties and responsibilities in modern society. There is a grave danger in the push towards legislative recognition of subjective rights (so called) in response to the demands of politically influential pressure groups.

A duty-centred society is preferable to a right-centred society. If individuals are concerned about their duties, responsibilities and obligations, they cannot be concerned about the rights, needs and freedoms of others. A right-centred society is one in which individuals assert their rights. People are encouraged by individuals, organisations and, State departments and instrumentalities, to demand rights, with no consideration for the effect of these demands on other people. Governments and pressure groups which focus on rights, give no thought to how rights can operate in the absence of a climate in which the importance of duties is emphasised. By comparison a duty-conscious society gives rise to respect for rights.

There is no end to the so called rights which can be demanded. A right-conscious society in effect recognises a few rights and neglects many others. The rights that are recognised are those which are demanded by the powerful, the aggressive and the nasty. There cannot be a right without a duty. Our moral and spiritual decay is at the root of all other problems. The major political parties, government servants and statutory employees, the media and educationists are not seriously confronting this decay. There are some religions men among the above who are conscious of the problems but are oppressed by the secular institutional structures. This minority is confronted by some who are totally antagonistic to moral and spiritual values, as well as those who profess commitment or who are nominal religious men, but at the same time, pursue and promote secular ideas, ideologies and goals which indirectly if not directly, undermine the spiritual and the moral. The latter are unaware of the effects of their actions. There is no indication that Government, the educationists or the media have any answers to our problems.

33. SECULARISM IN INDIA

India has been declared a secular state by its written Constitution and it is the duty of every Indian to standing for it and believe in this declaration. And yet recent political and social events have questioned this declaration. Is India a secular country only on, paper or does secularism actually exist in India, or is in the form of pseudo-secularism, a term the BJP and its allies seem to repeatedly harp on.

During the freedom struggle, secularism was emerging as the most dominant principle. The leaders of the Indian National Congress, Gandhi, Maulana Abul Kalam Azad, Nehru and others were deeply committed to the ideal of secularism, though each expressed it in very different terms. Secularism became the mantra of the Indian nation, a nation exhausted by partition and sectarian riots and above all, the assassination of Gandhi, did not want any more divisive talk. The founding fathers represented the aspirations of the different sections of society and it is due to the struggles of these different people that secular principles got enshrined into the Indian Constitution.

Under Jawaharlal Nehru and later under his successors in the Congress Party, the concept of a secular nation-state was officially adopted as India's path to political modernity and national integration. In the post-Independence scenario the social dynamics was very complex. The process of secularisation/industrialization was going on at a slow pace. Even at this stage, though the Constitution was secular, the state apparatus, the bureaucracy, the judiciary, the army and the police were infiltrated by communal elements. The Congress government, though predominantly secular, had many leaders in important positions that were influenced by a Hindu communal ideology. This resulted in a social development that was mixed; on the one hand, secularism thrived and, on the other, though communalism remained dormant, it was never dead. With the social changes of the late 70s and the early 80s, communalism got a strong boost and it started attacking secularism in a big way.

Today, the biggest challenge to the Indian nation is coming from forces claiming to represent the mainstream majority. There is an emergence of extremist voices that claim to speak for Hindus and they are laying down demands that threaten the idea of secular India. The biggest area of concern is that the state has emerged to be complicit, as an actor and player in mounting this challenge to Indian pluralism, which goes under the name of Hindutva.

The communal forces are actively propagating the myth that Secularism is a new mask of fundamentalism. They denigrate the secular policies, which are a hindrance to Hindu Right's unobstructed march to subjugate the oppressed in general and minorities in particular. They are equating fundamentalism with Islam, and the policies of Indian rulers with secularism, and appeasement of mullahs as being synonymous with secular policies. Further, Hindutva forces accuse that secularism pampers the Muslims as a vote bank. The Muslims are accused of extra-territorial loyalty because they allegedly cheer for Pakistan whenever India and Pakistan play cricket. Since Muslims are being thought as synonymous to fundamentalism, therefore, the assertion that the Indian state is appeasing fundamentalists in the name of secularism. It is precisely on this charge that the Father of Indian Nationalism, Mahatma Gandhi, was assassinated by one of the votaries of Hindutva.

The Christians, who are much lesser in number, are accused of being more loyal to the Vatican, another outside force and of trying to convert poor Hindus with inducements of education and food.

The fact, however, is that the social and the economic conditions of the Muslim community is dismal. If all the opportunist political policies of various governments have struck compromises, it has been with certain religious leaders of the minorities and the minorities have been kept in abysmal conditions. In that sense, the government policies have been anti-oppressed rather than pro-Muslim. Further, the fact that 130 million Muslims decided to stay back in India rather than joining Pakistan, should settle their status as true citizens. In the end, secularism begins in the heart of every individual. There should be no feeling of "otherness" as we all have is a shared history. Ours is a society where Sufis and Bhakti saints have brought in a cultural acceptance for each other.

34. WHY I GOT INTO MEDICINE?

Throughout medical school I tried to be involved in research and attempts at trying out new ideas, either in the lab or working with human subjects.

What interests me most is a path that combines the two, and one way to make that possible is to be an academic physician. I have always wanted to work in a teaching hospital or an academic institution, one that would give me the opportunity to take care of patients, give me the time and resources to carry out trials to present them and to be able to interact with trainees. I hope to develop the career of an academic oncologist and the aspect that has captivated me the most is that of drug development.

Any major change in oncology, at least for medical oncologists, involves the invention and discoveries of new drugs and every single one of these has to be tested in the setting of a phase I trial. In order to develop a successful career as an academic oncologist, one needs to be able to conduct well-designed clinical trials and to be able to publish reproducible respected genuine papers. I also strongly feel that quality is more important than quantity in terms of final outcome of all the efforts and work. I hope to be working in this field in the future and be able to carry out my ideas and implement the same and in the process make some contribution in the care of the cancer patient.

A major hurdle in this academic career that I hope to have is going to be the lack of expertise in the designing, implementation and evaluation of clinical trials. Medical school, residency and fellowship training are sadly lacking in this aspect. This I believe is not the fault of any particular institution but of the system in general.

Although every institution will have people doing very good work, both in the lab and the clinic, there is no incentive or drive to train or mentor the trainee in this aspect. I feel highly inadequate in this regard prior to embarking on this career track. The clinical research training programme, I feel, has the right topics and curriculum to help me overcome my weakness and lack of knowledge in this aspect. The prospect of having a formal training in this field and one that is so intense and diverse, is exciting and I would greatly appreciate the opportunity if given to me.

I am very confident that I will find it interesting, a great learning experience and I will be able to put it to good practical use in my career. I will have a sense of achievement if I can use what I learn here, while I am taking care of patients, or in a clinical trial which I have successfully designed and implemented with the knowledge and expertise gained here.

35. SOCIAL ENVIRONMENT

Social environment is influenced by one's power and wealth. This, in turn, determines success or failure in people's lives. If one born with a silver spoon in his mouth, he would easily be able to attend a fancy school no matter how intelligent he is or have any luxury he wants just because of power and wealth.

On the flip side, if one born to a poor family in a bad neighbourhood infested with violence and drugs, he would have much smaller chance of succeeding in life, more especially, going to an upper-class school. It is hard for many poor to go to college because of such high tuition fees.

Scholarships are available, but, even though one shows financial need, one still has a high grade point average and test scores. Even if one has a good mind, trying to study in a gang-ridden neighbourhood with constant gunfire isn't easy. With both parents working two jobs, there isn't any parental guidance. Whereas, the affluent, even if busy or working, have means to insure that their children are supervised and well taken care of. The rich also have the luxury of affording special tutors to help their children while other children are on their own.

It is common knowledge that it is difficult to get out of a bad situation such as growing up without any of the advantages others have, but many have managed. There is a way out, it just takes a strong mind and a strong will to do so.

If someone is intelligent enough, they can try to go out and grab the recognition they deserve. Social environment as a determining agent is definitely a human-made force. In society, the poor are regarded with contempt or completely ignored while the rich are seen as having the authority over everything. The poor are seen as undeserving, therefore, not receiving much of an education. In any society, there are always the strong and the weak, and, in this case, the weak are portrayed as the poor by the rest of the society.

Some feel that the weak in our society should be eliminated because they are no more than mere pests, irritating the rest of the society.

In my opinion, there isn't much to be done to change the way society thinks. As long as the elite control businesses and schools, they will still have the authority over what the public thinks and does.

If one never gives up, one can achieve his goal no matter how unreal it may seem at the time. The most important thing is never to let society get in the way. One must not fall prey to society's evils and give up.

If there were to be a solution, it would have to be bringing more jobs back into this great country of ours. Too many people are out of work because the greedy owners of companies are taking jobs away from local workers and giving them to outsiders who are paid next to nothing for intense labour. There is also a lack of good, well-educated teachers. Many of the bad neighbourhoods, where the above-mentioned lower class lives, are uneducated because there is a shortage of teachers to give them guidance. If schools were cleaned up and rid of all the violence, then more teachers would be willing to teach there.

36. AIR POLLUTION

Air pollution is a major problem facing our environment today. This dilemma is harmful to every single living creature on this planet.

Air pollution is all around us. It might not be as clearly visible in some areas as others, but the fact is that air pollution is still there affecting us in some way, shape, or form. It has been known to cause illness or death. Many people are not aware of this fact. There are two main causes of air pollution. One of the main causes is natural pollution. Natural pollution is windblown dust, pollen, fog, etc. The other main cause is people pollution. People pollution is the chief concern and the most serious form.

Most of the pollution is caused by industry, cars, trucks, and airplanes. The causes of air pollution go on and on. There are residential causes and industrial causes. Residential causes are those such as automobile emissions and forest fires. Industrial causes are those such as factory emissions and the burning of fossil fuels. One residential cause is the emissions of automobiles. This is probably the most harmful cause. People drive cars every day to get from point A to point B. If automobiles did not exist, the air would most likely be cleaner but then we would not be able to travel long distances in short periods.

Motor vehicle emissions are generated in several different ways and locations during engine/vehicle operation. The most important sources are, of course, those produced in combustion and vented through the exhaust pipe.

Industries that are the major pollutants include petroleum refining, metal smelting, iron and steal mills, grain mills, and the flour handling industry. The most common chemical natured factory pollutant is methylene chloride. The burning of fossil fuels is a major cause of air pollution. Fossil fuels are formed from the remains of ancient plant and animal life such as coal and natural gas. If complete combustion of fossil fuels was possible, it would only produce heat energy, water vapour, and carbon dioxide. However, this is not possible because the level of oxygen is never ideal, carbon monoxide forms of it.

Air pollution, as like any other pollution,

is harmful for the environment. Unlike other pollutions though, air pollution is not always visible in the environment. Air pollution is the cause of acid rain, smog, and creating holes in the ozone layer. Acid rain damages living organisms and materials. Deposition from acids, such as surphuric acid, and nitric acid mixes with the rain and goes into the soil and bodies of water. This is most common where burning of fossil fuel is highly concentrated. Acid rain is killing lakes. It can scar the leaves of hardwood forests, wither ferns and lichens, accelerate the death of coniferous needles, sterilise seeds, and weaken the forests to disease, infestation, and decay. Below the surface the acid neutralises chemicals for plant growth, strips others from the soil and carries them to the lakes and literally retards the respiration of the soil. From this you can see that biological damage is most pronounced in forests and lakes.

37. THE MOON

The moon is the only natural satellite of earth. The moon orbits the earth from 384,400 km with an average speed of 3700 km per hour. It has a diameter of 3476 km, which is about ¼ that of the earth. The moon is the second brightest object in the sky after the sun. The gravitational forces between the earth and the moon cause some interesting effects; tides are the most obvious. The moon has no atmosphere, but there is evidence by the United States Department of Defense and the Clementine spacecraft shows that there maybe water ice in some deep craters near the moon's North and South Pole that are permanently shaded.

Most of the moon's surface is covered with regolith, which is a mixture of fine dust and rocky debris produced by meteor impact. There are two types of terrain on the moon. One is the heavily cratered and very old highlands. The other is the relatively smooth and younger craters that were flooded with molten lava. Throughout the 19th and 20th centuries, visual exploration through powerful telescopes has yielded a fairly comprehensive picture of the visible side of the moon.

The hitherto unseen far side of the moon was first revealed to the world in October 1959 through photographs made by the Soviet Lunik III spacecraft. These photographs showed that the far side of the moon was similar to the near side except that large lunar maria were absent. Craters are now known to cover the entire moon, ranging in size from huge, ringed maria to those of microscopic size. The entire moon has about 3 trillion craters larger than about 1 m in diameter.

The moon shows different phases as it moves along its orbit around the earth. Half the moon is always in sunlight, just as half the earth has day while the other half has night. The phases of the moon depend on how much of the sunlit half can be seen at one time. In the new moon, the face is completely in shadow. About a week later, the moon is in first quarter, resembling a half-circle; another week later, the full moon shows its fully lighted surface; a week afterward, in its last quarter, the moon appears as a half-circle again. The entire cycle is repeated in each lunar month, which is approximately 29.5 days.

The moon is full when it is farther away from the sun than the earth; it is new when it is closer.

When it is more than half-illuminated, it is said to be in the gibbous phase. The moon is waning when it progresses from full to new, and waxing as it proceeds again to full. Temperatures on its surface are extreme, ranging from a maximum of 127°C (261°F) at lunar noon to a minimum of -173°C (-279°F) just before lunar dawn. The harvest moon is full moon at harvest time in the North Temperate Zone, or more exactly, the full moon occurring just before the autumnal equinox on about September 23. During this season the moon rises at a point opposite to the sun, or close to the exact eastern point of the horizon.

Moreover, the moon rises only a few minutes later each night, affording on several successive evenings an attractive moonrise close to sunset time and strong moonlight almost all night if the sky is not clouded. The continuance of the moonlight after sunset is useful to farmers in northern latitudes, who are then harvesting their crops. The full moon following the harvest moon, which exhibits the same phenomena in a lesser degree, is called the hunter's moon. A similar phenomenon to the harvest moon is observed in southern latitudes at the spring equinox on about March 21.

38. EFFECTS OF POVERTY

All over the world, disparities between the rich and poor, even in the wealthiest nations is rising sharply. Fewer people are becoming increasingly "successful" and wealthy while a disproportionately larger population is becoming even poorer. There are many issues involved when looking at poverty. It is not simply enough, or correct, to say that the poor are poor due to their own, or their government's, bad governance and management.

In fact, you could quite easily conclude that the poor are poor because the rich are rich and have the power to enforce trade agreements, which favour their interests more than the proper nations. This is a very serious problem in our society today. Poverty is everywhere and it needs to reduce so that our economy will be more stabilised and balanced that it has been.

A strong economy in a developing nation does not mean much when a significant percentage or a majority of the population is struggling to survive. Development usually implies an improvement in living standards such that a person has enough food, water, and clothing, a stable social environment, freedom, and basic rights to have fair chance for a decent life.

Poverty expands and its definition changes in accordance with temporary exigencies, including the interests of those who propound the definitions do the counting, which means that there is no concrete definition of poverty, except for the numbers.

Higher standard of living also attracts immigrants, which makes it hard for people living in urban areas to find good paying jobs, because the immigrants will work for lower wages. What about the myth that America is the land of opportunity? With such a high standard of living, many believe this is not true. Those who work hard and have the opportunity to be financially successful are rewarded with healthy, enjoyable lifestyles, while those who are disadvantaged and cannot receive these opportunities are punished and miserable. Disadvantaged does not mean those who are on welfare, or those who are too lazy to find work. People who have disabilities that make it hard for them to find jobs, and those who are born into poverty, cannot escape it and must be tortured and remain helpless until a solution to this social problem is reached.

To reach to a solution to this problem, I think that there should be more opportunities for those who are not able to receive proper education and training to receive good paying jobs. I think that employers should offer specialised training to employees so that they can further their knowledge of different positions and to move up in their companies. Hopefully, society will view those who suffer at the hands of poverty in a less discriminating way. Our nation must realise that because they may be poor, it does not mean that they don't deserve the same chances in life and are less of a human than those who have financial freedom.

39. RAIN FORESTS ALL THE WAY

The discussions these days are why are the rain forests depleting? Well, this research will help change the opinions of many people. Some facts about rain forests are. Tropical rain forests occupy about 7 percent of the earth's surface but harbour as much as 50 percent of the world's plant and animal species.

Also about 57 percent of all rain forests remaining are in the tropics in the western hemisphere: 30 percent are in Brazil. At the current rate of deforestation, tropical rain forests could be wiped out in 177 years. Less than 5 percent of the world's tropical rain forests are protected within national parks and reserves. Rain forests are becoming very scarce and should be taken into concern because depletion of rain forests is a problem.

One method of cutting down rain forests is slash-and-burn agriculture. Grant defines slash-and-burn agriculture as "Smallholders that are cutting down four or five acres of forest and set it on fire. The resulting ash fertilises the soils, which are notoriously poor in the tropics." Grant explains that now there are only charred stumps left, a lot of light reaches the ground and is oppressively hot. "In the past, a logger might take only a few trees per acre, while that would allow more light into the forest floor and raise the risk of fire." So when people decide to cut down forests, they are increasing the risk of fire. Rain forests have been burning up lately. An analysis of satellite by the EDF indicates that burning of rainforest land in Amazon increased 28% from 1996 to 1997. (Amazon Rainforest, 1) Research shows: "A total of 19,115 fires are reported from the NOAA-12 satellite images in the sample in 1996, while 24,549 fires appear in the 1997 data over the period."

One reason for rampant burning is that Brazil's environmental agency has no legal authority to enforce environmental law since 1989. A bill in the Brazilian Congress that would close the loophole passed the Senate earlier this year, but has been blocked by special interests in the Lower House. So of the reasons why the burning continues is because of the government, and the burning is increasing more and more because we need more land and crops.

Since the statistics show those rain forests are getting burned up, the government and people need to start taking concern towards the rain forest. The point of this essay was to persuade people as a whole to take rain forests into concern and act upon it. Some solutions to the problem are that the government should take greater responsibility and take control of the burning of the rain forests. Also the people can help the government out by understanding the needs of our rain forests.

40. THE DAMAGING EFFECTS OF ACID RAIN

Modern society is becoming overwhelmed with great amounts of pollution from cars, factories and an overabundance of garbage. The immense amounts of sulphur dioxide emitted into the air causes high levels of acid in the atmosphere. When this sulphuric acid is absorbed into moisture in the air, poignant rainfalls can be damaging to the external environment. Acid rain is destroying the world's lakes, air and ecosystem. Acid rain is killing lakes and decreasing the number of inhabitants in these fresh water bodies. Acid rain causes an ample deduction in the pH levels in water. At a neutral level the pH in water should be close to seven, yet in these acidic water bodies the pH levels can be as low as four. These pH levels of four contain more than ten percent acids than that of normal rain and one thousand times more acid than neutral water. Each decade the pH levels of lakes around Ontario have become ten times more acidic.

Acid rain causes traumatic effects in natural lakes and rivers. Acid rain causes air quality to deteriorate. As in water, acid rain causes the pH levels air to decrease. In the air, the sulphur dioxide, which diffuses into the air, mixes with moisture causing the pH levels to drop from the normal level. Again, the normal level is somewhere around seven, yet in some acidic air masses the levels can be as low as three. These lowered pH levels form a photochemical smog in the atmosphere. In the air nitrogen oxides react with ozone and some hydrocarbons in the presence of sunlight to form photochemical smog, the kind of yellow-grey haze which is literally alive and growing in stagnant air masses.

The ecosystem is slowly eroding due to the increased amounts of acid in the soil. Acid in the soil is causing the carbon dioxide respiration process to decelerate. On the other hand, plants to go through photosynthesis need carbon dioxide. When acid in the soil causing this soil respiration to slow down, in turn it causes the photosynthesis process to slow down. The soil also erodes when the pH levels drop. The acidic levels of the soil cause nutrients in the soils such as aluminium to break apart and the soil to erode. Soil erosion also causes a lower production of plants in the ecosystem. In the soil a process of decay called oligotrophication, means that fewer of the ions of acid are neutralised by the depleted biological community so the acid can cause further degeneration of natural processes, which in turn are less capable of combating the acid, and so on, in an accelerating process. Acid may obtrude fertilisation, stunt or kill the growth of seeds and make them sterile.

A second generation would be in danger of not being produced causing deforestation. Naturally the reduction of plants is causing the biological food chain to weaken. As smaller animals and insects feeding on these plants lose their food supply, they may also ensue death. In effect, the animals which feed off these animals ensure a decrease in their supply. In turn, humans may become starved if the acid rain effects increase.

Acid rain causes death of soil, plants and animals, affecting the ecosystem. Acid rain is becoming a major problem in our environment today. It is killing our fresh water lakes and its occupants. Also the quality of air is depleting, increasing the amount of smog and pollution in our atmosphere. Once the acid is absorbed in the soil, this puts the ecosystem in jeopardy of extinction. This is killing plants, animals, and soil, which is the basis of our existence. If this acid rain problem is not dealt with urgently, the natural world may be in hazard of demise.

41. GROW MORE TREES

Trees are tall plants with hard and thick stems, trunks. The main trunks of large trees like the mango and the banyan bear many branches, which further divide into smaller branches. Leaves grow on these branches. Branches cause the tree to spread out wide on all sides.

Trees are Nature's wonders and great gift to mankind as well as to all those who depend on it. While some dependents stay on the trees, others come to it to rest or to feed. Still others use them to raise their offspring. Humans have used many and almost every tree to their benefit.

It is very sad that the same humans are destroying trees all over the world in the name of "development". Create factories, new townships, wider roads, railways, entertainment centres and so on. They do not realise that they are committing a big mistake.

Trees are useful to us in many ways. Trees give us food such as fruits. These provide us with excellent nourishment. The wood from some trees such as teak, walnut, rosewood and oak is used to make furniture. Wood from other trees is used as fuel for cooking and for warming houses. Paper is made from wood and many trees are the source of useful modern medicines. The canopy of leaves and branches gives us shelter. Trees provide cool shade. Many trees, for example in a forest, can make the climate pleasant and the air clean. Forested areas get better rainfall compared to areas with no tree cover. When trees respire, they release oxygen that all animals need for their survival.

Most of the furniture in a house is made from wood. In mountainous regions, even the walls are made from logs of trees. In cold areas, where people need to heat their homes, wood from trees is used for heating. Many medicines are derived from trees. These include medicines for fever, malaria, heart-diseases, etc. By absorbing the extra carbon dioxide and releasing oxygen, trees help make the environment clean and more suitable to live in. Forested areas are pleasantly cool, get better rainfall and have cleaner air.

Many trees are grown especially for their products, such as the rubber tree, which gives us rubber that is so useful to us. Forests are dense collections of trees, plants, animals and birds within a small area of the earth. The Amazon rain forest is the biggest forest in the world. Many of the forested areas are protected by the national governments and converted into parks and wild life sanctuaries.

Large forests are fine-tuned ecosystems which can influence the climate and environment not only where they are, but also all over the world. For example, the forests all over the world are shrinking, thanks to the irresponsible felling of trees for "development". This is thought to be one of the most important reasons for global warming.

There is a lobby of governments, politicians, foresters, social scientists and environmentalists who vote for constructive development for the common good of the society. It seems prudent, for example, to remove a few trees that come in the way of construction of a 500-mile highway. At the same time, it is irresponsible to hack down a 70-year old teak tree just to get firewood for one's house. I fully agree with this kind of responsible forest management.

42. DEPRESSION AND TEENS

Teenage depression is a growing problem in today's society and is often a major contributing factor for a multitude of adolescent problems. The statistics about teenage runaways, alcoholism, drug problems, pregnancy, eating disorders, and suicide are alarming. Even more startling are the individual stories behind these statistics because the young people involved come from all communities, all economic levels, all home situations - anyone's family. The common link is often depression. For the individuals experiencing this crisis, the statistics become relatively meaningless.

Depression is a murky pool of feelings and actions scientists have been trying to understand since the days of Hippocrates, who called it a black bile. It has been called the common cold of mental illness and, like the cold, it's difficult to quantify. If feelings of great sadness or agitation last for more than two weeks, it may be depression. For a long time, people who were feeling depressed were told to snap out of it.

Depression, however, is considered a medical disorder and can affect thoughts, feelings, physical health, and behaviours. It interferes with daily life such as school, friends, and family. Clinical depression is the most incapacitating of all chronic conditions in terms of social functioning. Teenagers have always been vulnerable to depression for a variety of reasons. It's a confusing time of life because a teen's body is changing along with their relationships. Teenagers constantly vacillate between strivings for independence from family and regressions to childish dependence on it.

They're growing up in a world quite different from that of their parent's youth. Adolescents today are faced with stresses that were unknown to previous generations and are dealing with them in an often self-destructive way. Contemporary society has changed the perception of teenagers. New parental lifestyles, combined with changes in the economy, often give less time and energy for parents to devote to their offspring. Society often views teens for what they can be, instead of for who they are. Who they are becomes the identity of teenagers today. They are confronted with the ambiguity of education, the dissolution of family, the hostile commercialism of society, and the insecurity of relationships. This identity is fragile and is threatened by fears of rejection, feelings of failure, and of being different. Their sexual awakening comes in the age of AIDS, when sex can kill. In summary, teens today feel less safe, less empowered and less hopeful than we did a generation ago.

Depression is a common concomitant to this struggle. Depression is a growing problem amongst today's teenagers. Depression brings with it many problems that can be self-destructive. If a teenager has the benefit of early intervention and help in coping with his or her depression, however, the life script can be quite different.

43. PRIME MINISTER DR. MANMOHAN SINGH

Dr. Manmohan Singh, the 17th and incumbent Prime Minister of India, assumed office on 22nd May, 2004. He is the first Sikh Prime Minister of India. He also holds the distinction of being the first Prime Minister who has never been elected to the Lok Sabha.

Dr. Manmohan Singh was born on 26th September, 1932, in Gah, Punjab, in present-day Pakistan. His educational qualifications in economics comprise a master's degree from Punjab University (1954), an undergraduate degree from Cambridge University and a Doctorate Degree from Oxford University.

Dr. Singh, an economist by profession, served in the International Monetary Fund. He is acclaimed worldwide for his work at the United Nations. In the late 1980s he served as the Governor of Reserve Bank of India. In 1991 he was appointed as the Finance Minister by Prime Minister P.V. Narasimha Rao. During that period India's economy was going through a major financial crisis.

He hails from a poor farming background - his father owned a shop selling dry fruits, and the first time he ever wore a tie was for his first job interview. Manmohan Singh was so determined to get an education that he would study at night under streetlights, because there were so many people in the traditional, extended family home.

Dr. Singh, who says he became an economist because he wanted to eradicate poverty, studied at Oxford and Cambridge on scholarships. He wrote his Oxford doctoral thesis on India's export competitiveness. He later taught at the Delhi School of Economics and became a civil servant where he held a string of high posts.

In 1991, when Singh became the Finance Minister, India's economy was in a shambles. The country had an unsustainable fiscal deficit of close to 8.5 per cent of the gross domestic product - almost double of what it is currently. There was a huge balance of payments deficit. The current account deficit was close to 3.5 per cent of GDP and there were no foreign lenders who were willing to finance it. India had barely a billion dollars in terms of foreign exchange reserves - roughly equal to two weeks' imports. India was on the verge of defaulting on the repayments of its international loans.

In the last five years, somewhere in the haze of India's rapid economic growth and the glowing corporate performance, the spotlight turned away from the one man who years ago had almost single-handedly changed the way India's economy moved. Now Dr. Singh's time has come again. And he has a rather formidable reputation to live up to.

44. MEDIA AND CULTURE SIGN SYMBOL

A sign system is representation through communication which in turn leads to shared meaning or understanding. We hold mental representations that classify and organise the world, whether fact or fiction, people, objects and events into meaningful categories so that we can meaningfully comprehend the world. The media use sign systems through newspapers, magazines, television, internet, and the radio, etc. The conceptual map of meaning and language are the basis of representation. The conceptual map of meaning are concepts organised, arranged and classified into complex relations to one another. The conceptual map of meaning although allows you to distinguish your own individual interpretation of the world, at the same time, as holding similar views to that of other people in your culture, as the meaning is produced and constructed and in turn learned by a particular group of people.

If we have a concept of something in our minds we can say we know the meaning of this concept.

However, we cannot express or communicate this meaning without the second system of representation, language. Language is the only way in which meanings can be effectively exchanged between people, as people within the same culture are able to interpret the sign of language in the same manner. The media use these sign symbols so that an association can be made to the object, person, event, or idea, etc.

With this information of representation and language the media can familiarise people with many things, such as cultural knowledge. As advertising surrounds consumers, concern is often expressed over the impact on society, particularly on values and lifestyle. While a number of factors influence the cultural values, lifestyles, and behaviour of a society, the overwhelming amount of advertising and its prevalence in the mass media suggests that advertising plays a major role in influencing and transmitting social values. In his book *Advertising and Social Change,* Ronald Berman says: "The institution of the family, religion and education have grown noticeably weaker over each of the past three generations. The world itself seems to have grown more complex."

In the absence of traditional authority, advertising has become a kind of social guide. It depicts us in all the myriad situations possible to a life of free choice. It provides ideas about style, morality, and behaviour. While there is general agreement that advertising is an important social influence agent, opinions as to the value of its contribution are often negative. Advertising is criticised for encouraging materialism, manipulating consumers to buy things they do not really need, perpetuating stereotyping, and controlling the media.

The media must consider the cultural variables of each country, such as the complexity of learned meanings, norms, language, customs, tastes, attitudes, religion, traditions, education, lifestyle, values, and the ethical/moral standards shared by members of each society. These variables must be learnt by the media as not to offend the group they are portraying. Cultural norms and values offer direction and guidance to members of a society in all aspects of their lives.

45. WATER POLLUTION

The earth is facing a lot of environmental problems today, these problems are caused by humans. In search for the technology, humans begin to improve their lives without giving attention to what this development has caused to the other aspects of life on the face of the earth.

All aspects of life on the earth have been affected, as well as the sources of water. Sea and river pollution is one of the problems that resulted from the new technology, and humans should solve very fast to save our planet. Water is one of the most important sources of life on the earth a lot of animals live in seas, rivers and lakes. In addition, water is also important for humans, not just for drinking, seas are one of our main sources of food today, for example, sea food. Sea pollution has become one of the biggest problems facing our environment.

This pollution which is caused by the oil tankers or the oil spills could cause serious damage to the lives of many kinds of creatures that live in the sea. People were happy when the oil was first discovered. For them, it was a new source of energy that would help to made life a lot easier, no one ever thought that oil could cause so much damage, but it became clear when oil tankers began to dump oil into the sea.

The oil which was dumped into the sea for different reasons, could cause a lot of damage to the life in that sea, for example, a thick spot of oil could cover the surface of the sea and causes screening of the sun rays from the sea.

That screening can cause the death of many sea creatures, because most of the sea creatures depend on the sun for their lives. A lot of beaches are destroyed because of the oil spots, too. The oil spot finally ends up on the beach. A lot of birds that live on the beach will face death because they lost their source of food. People will be affected, too. A lot of fish will die so there will be no fishing. In some countries where they depend on sea water for drinking, they are going to have problems purifying. Rivers were facing the same problem, too.

The chemicals that have been used in manufacturing should not be dumped in lakes or rivers, because of the animals that live in these rivers and lakes. In some countries they polluted some of their big lakes because of the big factories that were built beside them in order to throw the waste of chemicals on these lakes, and the result was big loss of natural life. However, it is a big problem, we still cannot stop it from happening, but we can reduce it by enforcing stronger laws to stop these oil tankers.

46. INFLUENCES ON GOVERNMENT

Our governmental system is influenced by a number of "inputs" and factors that shape the outcome of political movements and decisions. These "inputs" include public opinions, political parties, interest groups, and the influence of mass media. They influence our government directly as well as indirectly. There is no need to mention that our government also uses these "inputs" for its own benefit.

The main issue that forms governmental decisions in a democracy is of course the public opinion. In order to be eligible to run for an office in our governmental system, one must be elected by the people or a representative thereof, and to achieve this task, one must listen to and obey the public's opinion. Therefore, the theory of democracy is most purely applied through election on behalf of the public opinion. Another important factor in our system of government are of course our political parties.

Parties enable the citizen living in a democratic society to establish a connection to governmental action and lead policy-making to his benefit or liking. Furthermore, a citizen can participate in society quite easily, since two party platforms which clearly indicate a party's goals and preferences. However, this democratic ideal does not always prevail. Parties can be influenced or even manipulated by people who contribute great amounts of funds to the party to have their own personal political wishes fulfilled which do not necessarily have to benefit society as a whole (power elite theory).

Interest groups account for an additional 'mover' in Washington. This political devise provides a supplement to our citizen's broad area of interests. Interest groups fill this gap and thus withhold the theory of democracy. Yet, 'Big Business' has found this devise to fulfil its political needs. Once again politics is influenced by small amount of citizens that own about two thirds of our nation's worth. Interest groups have grown more influential over the years and created a pluralistic society, in which people's everyday issues and interests are brought to the attention of our governmental system.

However, since there is a rapid growth in interest groups and political action committees, the competition among groups might become so extensive that demands on politicians might be too high and hence, our system would come to a halt or gridlock and nothing would be achieved anymore.

47. E-COMMERCE

An e-commerce solution for a business is the incorporation of all aspects of the business operation into an electronic format. Many well-established businesses have been selling on-line for years. For example, Dell Computers Corp. has been selling computers directly to end-users for years.

Currently, Dell is selling excessive of 1 million dollars worth of computers every day on the World Wide Web. When a business has incorporated e-commerce solution, the business will experience a lower operation cost while at the same time increasing its profit. The e-commerce solution will allow businesses to eliminate unnecessary paperwork. All paperwork and data can be transformed into an electronic format. Thus, it will eliminate valuable shelf space and data can be searched and accessed in a matter of seconds. E-commerce will also automate the sales process.

The administration department does not have to fill out any paperwork because the customer has done it already. Thus, the efficiency will be greatly improved. With an e-commerce solution, the business will be open 24 hours a day and 7 days a week. People from anywhere in the world with an Internet access will be able to visit the site at any time. They will not be restricted to the "normal" business operating hours. A "brick -- mortar" business is normally limited to serving the customers in its local geographical location. With an e-commerce solution, that business will not be limited to a geographical region, rather it opens itself to the global on-line market. Essentially, the business market exposure will be greatly increased. In conducting my study, I have researched extensively on the Internet for resources.

I chose the Internet as my primary research medium because e-commerce is still a fairly new technology. Since it is technology related, the Internet will provide the most recent data available. Printed publications will not be able to adapt changes as fast and efficiently as electronic publications. I researched many e-commerce related web sites along with some companies that conduct statistical studies.

Every smart business person knows, it is not what one knows, it is whom one knows. Passing out one's business card is part of every good meeting and every business person can tell more than one story how a chance meeting turned into the big deal. Well, what if one could pass out the business card to thousands, maybe millions of potential clients and partners, saying this is what I do and if you are ever in need of my services, this is how you can reach me.

Electronic publishing changes with one's needs. No paper, no ink, no printer's bill. One can even attach one's web page to a database, which customises the page's output to a database one can change as many times in a day as one needs. No printed piece can match that flexibility.

48. JUSTICE

In spite of being so strongly rooted in law and its related disciplines, the concept of justice continues to be elusive primarily because it belongs to both morality and law and at times the two may clash.

Initially justice was related to religion; people lived and died in the hope of divine justice and equity. But man's concern and involvement with the earthly temporal laws necessitated the formation of rules for the administration of authority and to help maintain law and order.

Ordinarily, justice should be viewed in its double capacity as reward for the good and obedient and punishment for the deviant, but, unfortunately, right from the beginning of human society, it has been associated with retributive or punitive punishment. Amongst the ancient Greeks, the Greek goddess Nemesis was the goddess of vengeance. This one-sided view of justice is also there because the wronged and the deprived clamour for it. Francis Bacon was wise enough to see this; he once commented that revenge is "a kind of wild justice".

But one must realise that this is not the only function of justice and men should see it only in relation to their wrongs.

It is difficult to identity law with justice. There may be times when the law may be strict and unfair, or may not cater to the exception. It may not cater to the human emotions involved and the legal justice may appear to be very lopsided to the ordinary viewer. For example, take the case of Shylock extracting his pound of flesh from Antonio in Shakespeare's *The Merchant of Venice.*

In this case, the law is being used for vindictiveness and not justice. It is the occasion of Portia's famous speech about justice and mercy where she says "earthly power doth then show likes God's when mercy seasons justice".

And even the law recognises the place of mercy as the innumerable interpretation of the same law leads one to believe. Shylock clamours loudly for justice but when the bond is interpreted literally as a pound of flesh and no more and no less, without a drop of blood, he waives his claim. Thus justice is for him a one-sided concept.

An eye for an eye, a tooth for a tooth, is the old punitive concept for justice rising out of anger, helplessness and the longing for revenge. This is not justice; it is merely retaliation and does not achieve much, for the past cannot be undone. It is true that in some cases it may act as a deterrent for men are deterred by fear of punishment. Men of the legal profession and psychologists are increasingly of the view that due attention should be paid to the factors and the pressures which may have influenced the behaviour of the culprit.

49. THE WORLD

The world is a messed up place and we all are stuck here until our lives are through, or until we choose to leave. It's strange that I go along with everything everyone tells me, such as that I should wear certain clothes or listen to certain songs. I often wonder why I do the things I do, but then I just realise that's who I am. People are confused about why they are here and they don't understand what life is supposed to be about. They think that there should be a certain way or think of a certain way, but all are wrong. We should all act however we want to and not let the world influence us.

Every day that I wake up I wish that the world would change to where it was all right to be who you really are. Instead you have got to be what the world wants you to be. It's sad that these days a child can be left out of a certain group because his parents cannot afford the outrageously expensive clothes that the other kids wear. This may cause the child to feel less encouraged to try in school or other activities. This is the kind of small thinking that causes a teen to act out in violence. After years of being picked on and labelled as a trouble-maker just because of who he or she is and were he/ she comes from. Society often blames parents or television for these tragedies because they cannot admit that their own selfishness and lack of respect for those less fortunate is spreading poison in the world. I once saw a man sitting on a street corner playing a guitar with his guitar case open. People passed him without looking or listening. Every now and then someone would toss some loose change or even a dollar, but they still never heard the music the man was playing. I stood and listened for about ten minutes to what was the greatest live version of "Free Bird" that I had ever heard. When the man finished I offered him some money not so people would see me doing, but because I thought his performance was well worth it. The man just smiled at me and declined it saying, "No thanks, your applauds are all the payment I was looking for." That was the moment in my life when I realised the world had it all wrong and society was blind.

There are so many possibilities and factors that could change the course of my life. Perhaps I will become a famous actor on the big screen, or a rich politician that will become president. One thing I know for sure is that I won't be one of those guys that live in the same town he grew up in, where everyone has known him since he was a little kid. You know the kind of guy that I'm talking about. One day they went to a college close to home and came back to be a teacher, coach, or manager of a furniture store. Don't get me wrong, these are all great people that make great parents, but that's not a life that I want for myself. I want to make a name for myself in this world, and in order to do that I got to do something big to get recognised and get out of this small town.

50. GREENHOUSE EFFECT

The greenhouse effect occurs when gases such as methane, carbon dioxide, nitrogen oxide and CFCs trap heat in the atmosphere by acting as a pane of glass in a car. The glass lets the sun light in to make heat but when the heat tries to get out the gases absorb the heat. The main gases that cause the greenhouse effect are water vapour, carbon dioxide and methane which comes mainly from animal manure. Scientists predict that if we continue putting the same amount of gas into the atmosphere, by the year 2030 the temperature will be rising as much as 0.5 degrees C (0.9 degrees F) or more per decade.

Over all the global temperature could rise anywhere from 5 to 9 degrees over the next fifty years. If the temperatures do rise as predicted several things could happen. The increase of temperature could alter the growth of crops in areas near the equator due to insufficient rain and heat. This could really hurt countries that rely on imported food. With the high temperatures the polar ice caps could melt and cause the sea water level to go up

1 to 3 feet. This increase could take out small islands, coastal cities and some shallow rivers.

The Everglades in Florida would be almost dead if not totally wiped right off the map. The Everglades is the home for many animals and plant life. If it did get flooded, they would all have to move northward across very dry land which they will not be able to endure for very long. When the hot temperatures do spread southward and northward, tropical diseases will spread with it.

Every day the satellite makes 500,000 measurements, each at a different place on the earth. Measurements are all made between 66 degrees north and south latitudes. The Cretaceous occurred over 100 million years ago. It was the warmest period we have knowledge of yet. There was so much carbon dioxide in the air that the oceans rose many metres. North America was flooded and split apart into two pieces. The temperature there was more than fifteen degrees greater than the average temperature today.

Scientists believe that the tilt of the earth's axis changes to tilt the opposite way every 10,000 years like a cycle. While going through this cycle it will change the climate of areas. Right now it is moving so that North America is going to be close to sun in winter. Seasons become more extreme when the opposite happens. This controls the cycle of ice ages. Volcanoes, when they erupt, send clouds of dust into the air blocking sunlight. This would cool the earth off more. Oceans are known to absorb carbon dioxide because of the ocean currents and the action of plankton. There is some evidence that there is naturally rapid climate change between each Ice Age, which confuses the whole global warming idea.

I think every human being should take part in the fight to stop global warming. The government is the key to this and they better do something soon or it will be too late. First, the United Nations should sponsor a meeting the nations of the world. They should establish a committee for handling the money, politics, and scientific research in order to help cut back the emission of gases into the atmosphere. Every country will contribute by donating money.

51. DISASTERS BRING OUT THE BEST AND THE WORST IN PEOPLE

The media keep disaster in the forefront of our minds. TV, radio and the front pages of the press seem to revel in disaster, whether natural or man-made, because the public have a morbid curiosity in it, providing it happens to other people. Disaster boosts TV ratings and sells newspapers.

As we absorb the results of a civil war, a famine, an earthquake, a hurricane, an air crash, we tend to put ourselves in the position of the victims and wonder how we would react. In such situations, most people act instinctively, and what they do is more spontaneous than calculated. That spontaneity is usually the subconscious reflection of character, and because life for most of us is lived on an even keel, how we behave in emergency is largely unpredictable, unless we have been previously conditioned to react in certain ways.

So what governs our reaction to an emergency? The answer is character. Character is governed by genetic structure, by upbringing and training, and by self-discipline, or its absence. If we react badly, we show cowardice, selfishness and indifference to the plight of others. If we react well, our conduct reflects the opposite of these feelings. In the latter case, genetic history alone may govern our actions, but in most cases, people are poised between good and bad. It is then that external conditioning will tip the scales in one direction or the other. Even more important than training is love, the kind which put others first and helps us to forget self. This is relatively easy where our nearest and dearest are concerned, more difficult and perhaps more admirable where the others concerned have no emotional claim on us. The old Latin tag *"amor vincit omnia",* love conquers all things, is most germane to our reaction to disaster.

The Second World War gave me a vivid example of two contrasting reactions to the same event. The house of a neighbour received a direct hit from a bomb which killed one of the daughters of the family. The father was a nice person. Most people would have shaken their fist at the skies over Coventry which were still full of German dive-bombers. Instead, he fell on his knees and prayed for the souls of the German pilots. The following day, what remained of his possessions lying round the shattered house were looted.

Two very different reactions to disaster. Looting often follows the breakdown of law and order. It is never justifiable, but it may be less reprehensible in some circumstances than others. Some would disagree, but they are those who have never seen a disaster such as a famine. If my children were crying for food and I had the chance to steal a bag of flour to make bread for them, I think I would steal the flour. Would this action reflect the best or the worst in me?

There is no worse disaster than war, and the trench warfare of 1914-18 saw perhaps the greatest slaughter of humanity of all time. Caught in machine-gun crossfire and by artillery barrages, hundreds of thousands of men were killed or maimed in a single battle. Yet there were countless examples of bravery and unselfishness on both sides when men would help the wounded or engage hopeless odds with total disregard for their own survival.

52. ADVERTISING

Advertising promotes more than mere products in our popular culture. Because images used in advertising are often idealised, they eventually set the standard which we in turn feel we must live up to. Advertisements serve to show us what the ideal image is, and further tell us the way to obtain it. Advertisers essentially have power to promote positive images or negative images. Unfortunately, most of the roles portrayed by women tend to fit the latter description.

The irony lies therein since it is these negative images which have been most successful in selling products. It is easy to understand the appeal which these ads hold for men, as they place women in an inferior role; one characterized by helplessness, fragility and vulnerability. Certainly one cannot deny that visual images serve to create the ideal female beauty within the material realm of consumer culture. The problem is that if one strays from this ideal, there's the risk of not being accepted by men. Advertisers, by setting ideals, not only sell their products, but in fact reaffirm traditional gender roles in mainstream.

Women portrayed in sexual ads are depicted as objects and commodities, to be consumed by men for visual pleasure and by women for self-definition. Any depiction of woman in scant clothing ultimately makes her look vulnerable and powerless, especially when placed next to a physically stronger man.

Studies show that advertisements will concentrate primarily on woman's body parts rather than her facial expressions. This distorted "ideal body image" is one of the leading causes for the recent rise of anorexia in young girls. The "waif" woman image is causing extreme low self-esteem for women of the times. The advertisement proves to be effective because normal women can never, and will never look like Kate Moss. All the hollow attempts will only bring more attention to these marketing strategies, and ultimately more business for Calvin Klein.

It is difficult to pinpoint the cause for Klein's overwhelming success despite the nature of his advertisements. Before Calvin Klein's waif image developed, it was thought that concentration on a woman's voluptuous physical features was what intrigued men. But this idea of Moss as a helpless child, with no real feminine curves at all, reiterates the argument that the male attraction to certain ads lies in the sexual power it gives them.

Women please men in their nudity, their purity, and their body size. Women can never be happy with themselves until their representation in advertising become more reflective of reality. But if the ads become more realistic, then the advertisements aren't able to sell their self-help images. Essentially the world of morals and advertising, if the two can logically coexist, form a constant vicious cycle.

53. COMMONWEALTH GAMES IN INDIA

The Commonwealth Games is a multinational, multisport event. Held every four years, it involves the elite athletes of the Commonwealth of Nations. Attendance at the Commonwealth Games is typically around 5,000 athletes.

The Commonwealth Games Federation (CGF) is the organization that is responsible for the direction and control of the Commonwealth Games.

The first such event, then known as the British Empire Games, was held in 1930 in Hamilton, Ontario, Canada. The name changed to British Empire and Commonwealth Games in 1954, to British Commonwealth Games in 1970 and assumed the current name of the Commonwealth Games in 1978.

As well as many Olympic sports, the Games also include some sports that are played mainly in Commonwealth countries, such as lawn bowls, rugby sevens and netball.

There are currently 53 members of the Commonwealth of Nations, and 71 teams participate in the Games. The four constituent countries of the United Kingdom, England, Scotland, Wales and Northern Ireland send separate teams to the Commonwealth Games (unlike at the Olympic Games, where the United Kingdom sends a single team), and individual teams are sent from the British Crown dependencies Guernsey, Jersey and the Isle of Man and many of the British overseas territories.

The Australian external territory of Norfolk Island also sends its own team, as do the Cook Islands and Niue, two states in free association with New Zealand.

The six teams that have attended every Commonwealth Games are Australia, Canada, England, New Zealand, Scotland and Wales. Australia has been the highest scoring team for ten games, England for seven and Canada for one.

At the 1930 games, women competed in Swimming and Diving only. From 1934, women also competed in some Athletics events.

The next edition is going to be held in 2010 in New Delhi, India. In 2014 the Games will be held in Glasgow, Scotland.

54. POWER OF YOUTH

Youth is the spring of life. It is the age of discovery and dreams. India has of largest youth population in the world today. The entire world is eyeing India as a source of technical manpower.

They are looking at our youth as a source of talents at low costs for their future super profits. If Indian youth make up their mind and work in close unity with working class people, they can hold the political power in their hands. Indian youth has the power to make our country from a developing nation to a developed nation. Is it a dream? No, their dreams take them to stars and galaxies to the far corners of the unknown and some of them like our own Kalpana Chawla pursue their dream, till they realise it and die for it in process.

The youth hopes for a world free of poverty, unemployment, inequality and exploitation of man by man. A world free of discrimination on the grounds of race, colour, language and gender. A world full of creative challenges and opportunities to conquer them. But let us convert these hopes into reality.

Unfortunately, no one is bothered to dream any vision. Martin Luther King has said, "I have a Dream" and the dream come largely true. If he had not thought of that dream he would have accomplished nothing in his life. Another problem is its indifferent attitude towards things, situation and politics. The new cool formula of "let the things be" is proving fatal to India's development.

Lack of unity and spirit is the major setback. In time, the youth, the students have to realize their power, their role, their duties and their responsibility and must stand up for their rights. Now it's time that instead of brain drain we should act like magnets and attract the world to India.

India can become a developed nation only if everyone contributes to the best of his or her capacity and ability. Youth is wholly experimental and with the full utilisation of the talents of the youth, India will become a complete nation. Let us hope for the same.

55. WOMAN

Men and women have similar faculties and capacities. The difference of sex may assert itself in family relationship, but there is no reason at all for it to assert itself in emotional, cultural, political or commercial matters. The very idea of restricting women to work connected with the home is motivated by a desire to bring increased freedom to the male population. It has its roots in the perpetual clash between liberty and equality.

Men have enjoyed freedom over the ages simply because women were denied it. The Greek city states did not bestow any rights on women or on slaves. In both Eastern and Western societies, for centuries, the belief that woman's place is in the home has been perpetuated. The myth of the fair sex or the weaker sex has proved a convenient peg on which to hang all kinds of inequality. Women had no independence or rights. In certain countries daughters could not inherit the property of their fathers, only male heirs were in direct line of succession and widows who had no sons had no right on ancestral property.

There have been a few cases of brave women who have struggled for their rights; but a full-fledged movement only began towards the close of the nineteenth century. It is only now, after years of struggle, that women in some parts of the world have left the confines of the house. They are coming forward to participate in the task of bread-winning and even in the defence of the country. There are woman scientists, administrators, executives, engineers, doctors, lawyers, judges and politicians. Though their numbers are still limited, their work has won them recognition. They now join the police not only as constables but also as officers. Even postal services employ women.

There are patches of matriarchal families in some societies and it is true that the greatest equality is enjoyed in those societies where the matriarchal system has prevailed. There is no possible reason for denying women these possible avenues of development. They have proven their merit and worth in almost all spheres of work. It is true that long working hours may interfere with their house-keeping and rearing of children; but advanced societies have begun to cater to this requirement. Many women give up their jobs for a few years to attend these important functions. When the children are a little older, they come back to work. With increased facilities and better gadgets at their disposal, housework has become less time-consuming than before.

Participation in the business of life is very important if we have a better society, a healthy home and men and women who are not frustrated and discontented. It would be an attempt to put the clock back if we were to differentiate between the sexes. It is impossible to make non-persons out of persons. In some ways women are even better workers than men. We have no right to discriminate against women.

56. "TO OVEREAT IS AS GREAT AS THE EVIL TO STARVE"

Eating is a matter of habit and upbringing. What one eats and how one eats depend on various circumstances. One may overeat when there is variety and abundance to go through as in a buffet dinner where people tend to overeat.

There are many evils of overeating. The organs are overtaxed. The stomach and the other digestive organs have to function beyond their capacity to help in digestion. As the digestive system is overtaxed, the needed energy does not reach the brain and so the person who always overeats is like a python. The efficiency will be low and slow and a person is not able to sustain long hours of concentration.

Obesity may be the result which again tells on the efficiency of the limbs and their movements. An obese person is again uncouth and ugly and becomes a laughing stock in public. Obesity leads to diseases like heart failure.

Then take a look at the cost of overeating. Because one overeats his bill of fare will be high. Again, by overeating one deprives another of his legitimate food. This is an important factor to be remembered by certain people who because of affluence do overeat. The excess food may conveniently be shared with those unfortunate ones who are not having enough food. Humanitarian societies help in the distribution of food to the needy people.

Overeating is a matter of habit. The parents have got a duty in teaching children to form good eating habits. They should not be given beyond their need. We have got a lesson to learn from animals which do not overeat and hence they keep up their energy and efficiency. We should not become a slave to our taste because our systems do not require so much of food.

If overeating is an evil, starving is equally bad because the organs don't get the necessary food for their efficiency. So we find people who are starved or semi-starved not as efficient as the well-fed people. This is economically bad for a nation, because starved people will get fatigued very soon and the quantum of work which they turn out will be less and so detrimental to the economy of the country.

Starved people suffer from anaemia, malnutrition and diseases connected with malnutrition. Semi-starved people continue to be a feature even today in certain countries where women and children suffer from malnutrition. They cannot resist diseases as the body's natural resistance becomes poor. So it is a drain on the nation's exchequer which has to meet a heavy bill in the form of hospitals. Death due to starvation has not been unknown. During famine millions of people have been wiped out but now with the advance of science and better transport system, death by starvation is reduced.

Starvation tells on the growth of children. Where children are starved, infantile mortality is very high. Starvation during pregnancy and postnatal period affects both the mother and the child.

While a person should avoid overeating, there must not be any ghost of a chance for starvation either. Providing enough food for people is every government's concern and all its economic machinery must be geared to that end. Dietary education is a must to save people front over-eating.

57. THE WAR AGAINST DRUGS

In this country, we are locked in a war we simply cannot win. We strive to protect over 15106.70 km (9387 mi) miles of border, against enemies who are driven by the lure of an obscene profit.

We have fought this version of war before, and have lost. All that has really resulted from this war is the overcrowding of prisons, the expansion of law enforcement's ability to encroach on the personal lives of ordinary citizens, and paranoia and distrust. I am referring to the war on drugs. As time goes on, it becomes more and more evident that the war on drugs is as useless as prohibition was almost 80 years ago. Now it has become a point of pride for our elected officials, who use the war as a re-election tool. To most people the fiscal reasons for ending the war are the most convincing.

Firstly, drug use or abuse is a medical and social problem but not a criminal problem, yet we think we're solving the problem by throwing people in jail. The logic seems to be, maybe if we just take their life away, confiscate all of their personal property, ruin their reputation and self-respect, put them in jail with the worst elements of society - murderers, thieves and rapists, when they will most likely be beaten or raped repeatedly they will see the error of their ways. It is not a very enlightened sentiment. Bear in mind, nicotine, caffeine and alcohol all are drugs. Nicotine is one of the most addictive drugs known to man, behind substances like heroin. Cigarettes kill over 300,000 people every year. Alcohol kills over 120,000 people every year. Alcohol has been linked to men beating their wives and children. In contrast, marijuana has a recorded history that dates back over 4000 years, and has never killed anyone in the direct way alcohol does.. The government spews propaganda as truth, to cover their collective backsides, which creates distrust and unrest, breeds contempt and disrespect in our children.

There is no way you will ever be able to eradicate drugs from this country without declaring martial law, doing house-to-house searches and increasing border security dramatically. The problem with drugs is not their effect; it is the corruption that is tied to the huge profits that doing illegal business commands. Increasing penalties for drug crimes will just increase the prices and thereby the profits for people willing to take the risk. Along these profits will come increased war in our neighbourhoods as gangs and dealers fight and kill for the enormous profits.

Supply is driven by demand. As long as there are people that want to adjust their state of mind, there will be someone to help them do it, and adjusting our state of mind is part of human nature. Go to a schoolyard and watch kids spin round and round till they fall down. Just as you can't cure a cold by taking cold medicine, you can't cure substance abuse by throwing people in jail. Substance abuse is a symptom of a larger problem, and we can't continue to pretend it doesn't exist.

We have driven ourselves into such a moral quandary that it will take years to fully recover. But our present course of action has proven to be more destructive than drugs themselves. Substance abuse (including over-eating) is people hiding from their problems. The only way we are going to stop substance abuse is by lowering the pressure in day-to-day life for our citizens.

58. ROAD SAFETY

It has been statistically shown that during the past five years, the number of fatalities and injuries associated with road accidents are steadily increasing. This type of carnage impedes the positive growth of our country and need to be stopped. Think about the most important factor that needs to be looked at in our goal to sustainable development is social responsibility. That is, drivers need to have a responsible attitude and a level of maturity when given this privilege. The attitude of drivers plays a major role in road safety. Drivers need to be cautious, and sensitive to the rules and safety regulations of the road. Safe habits need to be adopted and practised constantly. Drivers must take responsibility for their condition at all times.

Drivers who feel sick, tired, or upset should not drive during these periods. If drivers use corrective lenses, these should always be worn. All these are elements of social responsibility. It must be understood by all drivers that driving is the privilege of mature, responsible individuals who need to recognise that things such as these are potentially dangerous, if not taken seriously. Road rules such as speed limits and no parking zones also need to be strictly adhered by drivers. Due to drivers disobeying these simple rules, they significantly increase the risk of accidents and make it difficult for other drivers in the process. Typical examples of drivers practising very unsafe habits are drivers who cut people off in traffic, because they are in a hurry and drivers who make sudden lane changes or attempt to outrun yellow lights.

Drivers, however, are not the only ones to be blamed. Drivers cannot effectively drive safely in unsafe conditions. Roads should be properly maintained in order to function safely and efficiently as means of allowing transport to take place. Impediments on roads cause drivers to lose control over their vehicles and force drivers to make illegal moves. If impediments such as potholes, stones, tree branches, etc., restrict then our present drivers would need to infringe upon traffic flowing in the opposite direction in order to pass. Should these impediments be remedied, roads will be made safer to a significant degree.

Maintenance of infrastructure should also include properly functioning lights on roadsides for night drivers and properly maintained street signs and traffic directing arrows. Many accidents are caused due to improperly lighted streets.

Good infrastructure is a necessity in the area of safe driving. Areas of congestion are also common key locations of road injuries. Congestion tempts drivers to make illegal and dangerous turns, and violate road laws, and it also provides temptations such as overtaking in critical areas, such as intersections, which is definitely harmful and dangerous. Problems such as these can be solved by the introduction of traffic wardens in key locations who will regulate the passage of vehicles and thus ensure a smooth, freely flowing line of traffic which avoids putting temptation before drivers.

Another alternative is making the public aware about other routes which enable drivers to reach the same destination. This will altogether avoid the problem of congestion and reduce harmful road incidents.

59. WHY SMOKING IS HAZARDOUS?

Smoking is one of the most preventable causes of death in the world. Around 1.3 percent of all deaths in India have been due to tobacco consumption in 1990, and would rise to 13.2 percent by 2020.

Smoking has numerous other effects as well. It leaves you reeking of smoke, yellows your teeth and hands, can give you respiratory and cardiovascular problems, and cause you to leave on the street due to the fact that you broke. Smoking is an expensive habit. The average cost of a pack is Rs. 40 and an average smoker smokes a pack per day. In one year that's wasting in chores a lot of money.

The tobacco industry makes crores of rupees each year of addicted smokers. The company adds nicotine, which is addictive to their cigarettes to try and prevent you from not buying their products. The nicotine can raise your blood pressure, heart rate, and oxygen demand for muscles, mainly in the heart.

This causes you to need deeper breaths after

running or physical exercise and lessens your ability to perform well during sport activities. Secondhand smoke also affects others as well as you. Secondhand smoke comes from two places: smoke breathed out by the person who smokes, and smoke from the end of a burning cigarette. Secondhand smoke causes health effects, including cancer, breathing problems, and asthma. Secondhand smoke contains thousands of chemicals and a majority of them are poisons.

Secondhand smoke is responsible for between 150,000 and 300,000 respiratory infections in infants and children under 18 months. Around the same number of adults occur similar problems each year. About 37,000 non-smokers die each year because of it. A person who doesn't smoke married to a smoker has a 30% greater chance of getting lung cancer than the wife/husband of a nonsmoker.

When you stop smoking, you get your sense of smell and taste back, your cough goes a way you'll digest your food more ordinarily, feel more alive, it'll be easier to climb stairs, no yellow teeth from the build up of tar, no bad breath and no odour, and the most important thing is that you'll live longer.

Now there are programmes in your local areas to help you stop smoking. You can purchase over the counter smoking gum. It is never too late to quit so it is easier to quit now than later. I would not want this happening to me so that's why I'm against smoking. I told you that it could give you negative personal effects, is expensive to continue and can change your life. People might thinks it "cool" to smoke but it's really not. I hope this was a very persuasive speech and will surely make you convinced.

60. THE IMPORTANCE OF WATER

The life of both animal and plant, is impossible without water. Without water men can die of dehydration. About 70% of the human body consists of water. Of the total surface of the earth, 75% is water, and just below the surface of the land in most areas there is a saturated layer known as the water table. Animals and plants have large percentages of water in their make-up and some animals regulate their movements according to the water sources.

If there is no water there can be no life. The moon is a sterile desert because there is no water in it. It is to be remembered that it was water that determined the location of human settlements and without the Nile the Egyptian civilization would have not developed. The Nile provided the Egyptians facilities for irrigation and transport. As Herodotus said, Egypt is the "Gift of the Nile".

The urban man rarely thinks of the importance of water. When he needs water, all he has to do is to turn on the tap. The only time the urban folk becomes aware of the importance of water is when there is a drought and their water supply is irregulated. If water rationing becomes too drastic, they may find themselves in a worse position than the rural man who may have a steady supply of water from his well.

Imagine a day when the taps ran dry: Mr. Townsman would have found life intolerable. He could not brush his teeth, have his shave and could not take bath in the morning. After lunch, he had a very difficult time trying to wash up. He might have used cloth to wipe his crockery. He could not wash his car. At the end of the day, however, Mr. Townsman would have realized that water is precious and he should not be a water-waster.

Scientists find water the most fascinating fluid in the world because of its versatility and usefulness. Electricity is generated by the force of running water. Unlike other substances, water expands when freezing takes place. In ancient Rome snow was used to pack prawns and meat. Ice is used for refrigeration. Water is converted into steam and used as power.

Whatever man eats is dependent on water for its growth. Water can convert whole, barren tracts of land into luxurious, rich and fertile regions, through the use of irrigation. In parts of Spain, diminishing quantities of rain have caused fertile land to dry up in the past years, creating barren deserts. This in turn has caused many men and their families to move to new places.

Most of us who take our daily supply of water for granted, may not be able to fully appreciate the importance of water. Many have perished through lack of water.

In ancient times, military men knew that the most effective way of subduing any city or fortress was to cut its water supply.

61. CONSEQUENCES OF DRUNK DRIVING

People chose to drink and drive for numerous reasons. Sometimes people feel that they must drink to have a good time but have no intention of driving. This is not always how it turns out. Usually after one has drunk alcohol, his or her ability to make smart decisions has been impaired. So in the end they decide that they can drive. This decision may not always results in getting arrested or having an accident, but it is too great a risk to take. Drunk driving is a crime that has consequences that affect a person both personally and financially. If one is caught in the act of drunk driving he or she is often faced with a lot of fines. These fines include court costs, which can get into hundreds and the fine for the crime itself, which are very high in cost.

One gets into a wreck while drunk driving, his or her insurance probably will not cover the accident, which, depend on the severity of the accident, could cost an enormous amount of money.

Drunk driving is a crime that can cost one a lot of money, which could be used for education or other important things. It is a very bad thing to have the reputation of a person who gets into a lot of trouble. If one is like I am, he or she does not like people to think badly of them, and getting arrested is definitely not a positive event.

So in the end, the reputation of drunk driving could ruin his/her future. If one were to hurt another individual in his or her stupidity of drunk driving, he will have to live with it for the rest of his life. Say, someone was in the car when the wreck accrued and they got severely hurt or even killed, the driver of the car would feel responsible for that person. Even worse if two cars were to collide and one of the cars was being driven by a drunk driver, the sober driver is more likely to be injured. This is because a drunken person's body will remain limp throughout the wreck, whereas a sober person will tense up and be more likely to be injured.

The main reason that I have chosen to quit drinking, is because I do not want to mess up my life or someone else's life over something as stupid as drunk driving. I realise that what I have done is very wrong and dangerous, and not just because I got caught but I do not know how I would be able to live with myself if I were to kill someone. I would not want my loved ones deal with my deat I also do not want to make my parents go throug ny more grief than I already have. I realised that have more opportunities than many other peop to redeem myself, and I have chosen to take m good luck and change.

The personal and financial cost of drunk drivir are too great a risk to take. The many things that or can be charge with or have to deal with are reasor enough to quit the bad habit. Alcohol is a drug th can cause people to do irresponsible things that ca result in very expensive fines and personal anguis In conclusion, there is no excuse that can cove someone for making the unintelligent decision t drink alcohol and then drive a car.

62. BEASTS OF BURDEN

The abundance of nature's variety is perceptible in the world of animals. There are animals to meet man's requirements in the different regions of the world. Donkeys, mules, horses, camels, yaks, oxen and elephants are some of the animals used for pulling loads and carrying weights. Man's own capacity is limited and he can carry only limited weights for short distances. Other modes of carrying weight are comparatively recent in man's history. Now there are trains and trucks, boats and planes, trolleys and wagons; but this has not been the case in the past. Even when these are available, their utility and mobility may be limited. There are vast stretches of sand and narrow hilly terrains where man must depend on animals and where a motorbike or a motorboat are ineffective. In such cases it's nature's ingenuity which provides the answer.

Man's dependence on animals has always been there whether he used them for ploughing his field, for ferrying water, for travelling or for carrying loads. The camel is one such beast of burden. The Bedouins of Arabia call it "Ata Allah", i.e., God's gift. It justifies this epithet by coming to man's rescue when motors and machines fail. It is difficult for a person brought up in the lush. In the rich region of Malaysia or Singapore it is hard to imagine the vast endless stretches of sand in the wilderness of Sahara or of Thar desert. Camels have been carrying weight even since man made their acquaintance. The camel can go without water for long periods - if it is not working too hard. It can outlast a horse and can carry a load of more than two hundred kilos.

Mules are sturdy animals, and where donkeys or horses cannot find their way, mules are able to go along. Mountaineers and soldiers find them very useful for moving heavy equipment in the mountainous regions. In areas where the heavy monsoons easily flood the rivers, and boatmen are afraid to ferry across, elephants can be used for ferrying loads and people across the river. With their heavy bulky bodies and tall stature they are able to withstand the strong current and can drift along diagonally to the other bank. In the snowbound areas of Tibet, Yaks are used for carrying loads. Their thick fur provides them with protection against the cold.

The most well-known beast of burden used by potters and woodcutters, and an important character in many fairy tales, is the donkey. Dull and stupid, the donkey is a common enough sight in some countries. Associated with stubbornness, the poor beast is often given a bad thrashing for this trait. These animals which help man carry loads have been responsible for the beginning of trade and merchants have carried their goods and travelled on them from one country to another. They were also used during wars, especially horses and elephants. Now man has eliminated and rendered superfluous their help in some areas but it is not possible for him to do so entirely. The bullock cart and the horse-drawn carriage have still their glamour and utility.

63. VIOLENCE IN SPORTS

With the increase in society taking a stance against violence by many people, sports has become an area where some feel that the violent acts such as the hitting and fighting that occurs should be eliminated. You cannot change something that has been around for so long because it would change the aspect of the game to something completely different.

The elimination of violence should not be done in sport because the violence is a part of the game which would only hurt its popularity. The reasons that violence is occurring in sport is due to six theories according to John Schneider. "The violence in sport mirrors the violence found in society, violence as the result of economic incentives, the influence of crowd behaviour on player violence, genetic causation for player aggression, learning theory and player aggression, and psychological stress." The theories of sport mirroring society, violence as a result of economic incentive, and the influence of the crowd behaviour are the theories that I feel are responsible for the increasing violence in sports.

Most people when involved in a highly stressful situation where violence is around would probably resort to a fight to resolve their differences. In sport, why should we expect any difference? In events such as hockey games, where people are expected to hit and make body contact, sooner or later a fight will break out and the fans will yell and scream for their favourite players involved. Like anything, if people around us are applauding us for a certain act we have done, we will try to do it over so that we will continue to be praised.

"The emphasis in formalised sport on victory may, in fact, promote deviant behaviour and poor sportsmanship." I totally disagree with the above quote because being an athlete myself, I can never recall a time when I could have related my deviant behaviour to my sporting past. Sports does not promote poor sportsmanship, it creates a drive to succeed within yourself and try to do the best at whatever you do whether it be in sports, school or at a job. The violence that is occurring today is not occurring more than it was ten or twenty years ago like some people might suggest, it is only being shown and talked about more by the mass media. If there is one group to blame for the increase in violence I feel that it would be the media and not the athletes. If you turn on the television to watch a sportscast, it will always glorify an act of violence like a "hit of the night" or repeat of some type of fight whether it be in hockey, boxing or a bench-clearing brawl in baseball. I can recall on numerous occasions where the media has hyped up a hockey game involving two "tough guys" and creating a hysteria in sporting world wanting to see the outcome of the fight.

64. CAUSES AND CONSEQUENCES OF EROSION

Erosion is the eating or wearing away of land features. It is caused by a variety of factors, some natural and others man-made. The consequences can be serious both for the natural world and for man himself.

The natural causes are weathering, water, ice, wind and change of temperature. The changes may be very gradual, sometimes taking millions of years and dating back to the major upheavals of the planet when the earth was very young. Wind and rain driving incessantly against sandstone, formed originally by immense pressures on early sea-beds and then lifted above sea-level by volcanic eruption or the clash of land-plates, wears the stone back into sand, thus creating beaches along the seashore. In the case of harder rock such as granite, surfaces are worn smooth.

Weathering also erodes exposed coastlines in temperate zones. Often cliffs and dunes simply disappear over perhaps a short period of two or three hundred years. The sea encroaches, and sometimes coastal villages are lost. There is written evidence of English villages having been lost under the waves.

The sea plays an important role in the erosion process. The Netherlands, facing the turbulent North Sea, have for centuries fought the battle against salt water encroachment due to erosion. Great dikes have been built to exclude the sea, and gradually the low-lying salt flats have been sweetened and fertilised for agriculture and bulb-growing. In another way, the sea also erodes rock fragments by friction due to the tides. The smooth pebbles on northern beaches are the result of their having rubbed together over millions of years.

The great ice-floes attached to the poles play a conspicuous part in regulating sea levels. In general, sea levels are thought to be rising, though opinions vary as to the rate. At present, the fear factor in greenhouse effect is punching of holes in the ozone layer due to industrial gases and use of CFCs. Nations are beginning to agree to eliminate these hazards. The result might be the melting of ice-caps causing a devastating rise in sea levels. This would put much of the land in temperature climates under sea-water.

Slow-moving glaciers also have an effect. Their immense power pulverizes any rocks in their path. The piles of shale at the foot of many mountains resulted from the pressure of glaciers millions of years ago.

Wind is probably the greatest single cause of erosion. Where there is no protection given to the soil, and after a period of drought or intense heat, the soil crumbles to dust and literally blows away. Man himself can either let this happen or take steps to prevent it. Rain, of course, has a dual effect. In some circumstances, it can wash away the soil into river beds, where it is carried down to estuaries, often silting them so that they require dredging. In land, and on flat territory, rain holds the soil together. Yet, rain depends on trees and foliage which cause clouds to precipitate. In USA, the central plains of North America from time to time become dust bowls, simply because all vegetation has been cleared in favour of large-scale and economic cereal growing. The same clearance of rain forests goes on currently in South America in favour of cash crops. Conservationists throughout the world are resisting these clearances, but are fighting vested interests.

65. ARE MOBILE PHONES ESSENTIAL OR DANGEROUS?

Mobile phones are considered as an essential part of modern day life, from the business person who uses the mobile phone as a vital link with the office, to the teenager who has the phone for recreational purposes.

Mobile or cellular phones have changed dramatically over the past two or three years. The new generation of WAP phones now allow the user to connect to the Internet, send e-mail and even listen to the radio. The new e-mail feature is a tremendous advancement in technology, that allows businesspeople to contact their office at anytime day or night. Sending e-mail is not nearly as expensive as the conventional methods of contact, therefore, it has the potential to reduce costs considerably for the company.

The reduction in costs associated with owning and using a mobile phone is largely due to the introduction of the new pay and go tariff which means that many more people are now able to afford a mobile phone. The main disadvantage of this is that the networks can become overloaded and make it extremely difficult to connect the network. The consequences of this could be disastrous; mobile phone owners are lead to believe that they can contact help in the event of an emergency when needed though in effect the crowd network may make this impossible.

The public have a choice whether or not to subject themselves to the potential risks of using a mobile phone, yet this freedom is taken away when a transmitting mast is erected outside a school or close to their own home. With the experts unsure at present whether transmitting masts pose a health risk, especially to children under the age of fifteen, the ease at which telephone companies can site and erect these masts is, at best, irresponsible.

Another danger associated with the use of mobile phones is that of drivers using them while driving. Recently scientific evidence has suggested that the radiation from the handsets can cause temporary memory loss, although there is only one in five million chance of this occurring. With the risk being so slight, many will choose to dismiss this but what if this memory loss causes a driver of a car or another vehicle to crash and injure a family member or friend?

Even if mobile phones are found to be dangerous, will they be stopped being used? For many years it has been widely acknowledged that smoking causes cancer, still many people continue to ignore government health warnings and continue to smoke and many more people choose to start smoking every week. With the mobile phone becoming ever more affordable, will the people stop making its úse because it is found to shorten their life expectancy, or will the same happen as happened with cigarette warnings? Many people defiantly will stop using their mobile phones. Others, particularly those who depend on their mobile phone to communicate with friends or business people, will not stop. One of the ways that the government have attempted to discourage people from smoking is to ban all cigarette advertising. This strategy could be applied to mobile phones in a way that prohibits mobile phone companies from targeting the younger generation. The government could also insist that mobile phone manufacturers include health-warning leaflets with each phone sold.

Substantial research supports the conclusion that the radio signals emitted by mobile communication equipment present no health risk. Periodic review by numerous government agencies, international health organisations and scientific bodies support the observation that the radio signals from mobile phones and other portable communications devices pose no health risk. The scientific consensus drawn from the weight of evidence accumulated over many years is clear. There is no evidence that the radio signals generated by mobile phones, transmitting masts or other portable communications devices pose a health hazard. The above evidence in my opinion provides a sound basis for concluding that mobile phones are safer to use and plays an important role in every individual's life.

35.	English Grammar Easier Way	160/-
36.	General English for Competitive Examinations	160/-
37.	Spoken English	150/-
38.	School Essays, Letters Writing and Phrases	125/-
39.	How to Write & Speak Better English	150/-
40.	Quote Unquote (A Handbook of Famous Quotations)	175/-
41.	Improve Your Vocabulary	150/-
42.	Common Errors in English	150/-
43.	The Art of Effective Letter Writing	150/-
44.	Synonyms & Antonyms	150/-
45.	Idioms	150/-
46.	Business Letters	125/-

Unit No. 220, 2nd Floor, 4735/22, Prakash Deep Building,
Ansari Road, Darya Ganj, New Delhi- 110002
Ph.: 23280047, 9811594448
• E-mail : lotuspress1984@gmail.com, www.lotuspress.co.in